CONNECTIONS

Creating Meaningful Relationships
In a Disconnected World

by

Robert N. Jacobs
MSC

All rights reserved
Copyright © Robert N. Jacobs, 2025
The right of Robert N. Jacobs to be identified as the author of this
work has been asserted in accordance with Section 78
of the Copyright, Designs and Patents Act 1988
The book cover is copyright to Robert N. Jacobs
This book is published by
Growth Seeker Publishing Ltd.
www.growthseekerpublishing.com

This book is sold subject to the conditions that it shall not, by way of
trade or otherwise, be lent, resold, hired out or otherwise circulated
without the author's or publisher's prior consent in any form of binding
or cover other than that in which it is published and
without a similar condition including this condition being imposed
on the subsequent purchaser.
This book is a work of fiction. Any resemblance to
people or events, past or present, is purely coincidental.
ISBN: 9798281371193

To my daughter Ava, whose heart and boundless curiosity remind me every day of the beauty of genuine human connection. May you always find the courage to nurture meaningful relationships and the joy that comes from truly belonging.

"In a world where everyone speaks but few truly listen, let your connections be bridges of empathy, trust, and joy, because life's greatest moments happen when hearts genuinely meet."
Robert N. Jacobs

Foreword

In an age where connections seem abundant yet genuine relationships are increasingly scarce, Connections: Creating Meaningful Relationships in a Disconnected World is a timely and invaluable guide. It confronts the reality that you are fundamentally wired for connection and that your emotional, spiritual, and even physical well-being relies on the quality of your relationships.

Written with heartfelt insight by Robert N. Jacobs, this book explores the intricate dynamics that shape your connections, from recognising uplifting, energy-giving relationships to safeguarding your well-being against those who drain your vitality. Through practical guidance, grounded wisdom, and relatable experiences, Jacobs empowers you to cultivate emotional connectivity intentionally, transforming superficial interactions into bonds of genuine significance.

What makes this book uniquely valuable is that it doesn't merely offer a theoretical exploration of relationships; it provides actionable insights into creating the type of connections you deeply desire. You will learn how empathy, clear boundaries, and authentic self-awareness are foundational for healthy interactions, helping you build supportive communities and nurturing families. Each chapter is an invitation to strengthen your bonds, heal old wounds, and embrace meaningful relationships as a source of strength and joy.

As you delve deeper, you will recognise your tribe, the people who truly resonate with your core beliefs and inspire your growth. Jacobs guides you to foster resilience through the positive influences around you and gently leads you toward reclaiming your energy from negative interactions. By learning how to manage and elevate the energy within your relationships, you will unlock the transformative power of human connection, creating ripples of positivity that extend far beyond your immediate circle.

Whether you seek deeper friendships, more harmonious family dynamics, fulfilling romantic partnerships, or a positive professional environment, the insights in these pages will become indispensable. Reading this book will challenge you to look inward, inviting profound personal growth as you build stronger, more meaningful bonds.

This journey begins with a commitment: a decision to move from disconnectedness to heartfelt engagement. As you read, reflect, and implement these teachings, expect to see a profound shift, not only in your relationships but in your overall experience of life itself. Robert N. Jacobs has provided a compassionate, practical, and inspiring roadmap toward genuine human connection. You now hold the opportunity to create the fulfilling relationships you have always desired; embrace it.

Simona Gallotta

Life Coach & Author

Table of Contents

Chapter 1

The Foundation of Connections 1

    The Importance of Emotional Connectivity 2

    Understanding Energy in Relationships 3

    Identifying Your Personal Energy Signature 6

    The Psychology of Connection: Tribal Instincts in the Modern World 8

    The Spectrum of Social Bonds: From Acquaintances to Soulmates 10

    The Role of Empathy in Building Strong Connections 12

    Setting Boundaries: The Balance Between Giving and Receiving 15

    The Science of Vibrations: How We Attract and Repel 17

    Cultivating Self-Awareness to Enhance Connectivity 19

    The Power of Intention in Relationships 21

Chapter 2

Energy Givers: The Source of Light 25

    Characteristics of Energy Givers 25

    The Impact of Positive Energy on Your Life 27

    How to Attract and Recognise Energy Givers 30

    Nurturing Relationships with Energy Givers 32

    The Role of Gratitude in Relationships with Energy Givers 34

    Creating a Supportive and Uplifting Community 36

    The Ripple Effect of Positive Energy 38

Balancing Giving and Receiving 40

Learning from Energy Givers 42

The Long-term Benefits of Surrounding Yourself with Positive People 45

In Conclusion 47

Chapter 3

Energy Vampires: Recognising and Protecting Yourself 48

Identifying Traits of Energy Vampires 48

The Psychological Profile of an Energy Vampire 50

Setting Boundaries with Energy Vampires 52

Techniques for Shielding Your Energy 54

The Importance of Emotional Detox 56

Managing Relationships with Energy Vampires in the Workplace and Family 59

Healing from the Effects of Energy Vampires 61

Transformative Conversations: Dealing with Energy Vampires 63

The Role of Forgiveness in Releasing Negative Connections ... 65

Empowerment: Taking Back Your Energy 67

In Conclusion 69

Chapter 4

The Quest for Your Tribe 71

Defining "Tribe" in the Modern Age 71

The Significance of Finding Your Tribe 73

Steps to Discovering Your Tribe 75

Building Meaningful Connections within Your Tribe 77

The Role of Shared Values and Beliefs in Tribal Connections .. 79

Navigating Differences Within Your Tribe 81

Cultivating a Sense of Belonging 85

The Healing Power of Tribal Support 87

Evolving with Your Tribe 89

In Conclusion 91

Chapter 5

The Art of Connection in Family Dynamics 93

Understanding Family Energy Dynamics................................. 93

Healing Familial Wounds 96

Building Bridges: Improving Family Connections 98

The Role of Unconditional Love in Family............................. 100

Navigating Family Conflicts with Empathy 102

Setting Healthy Boundaries in Family Relationships 104

The Impact of Family History on Your Energy 106

Forgiving and Letting Go of Past Hurts 108

The Power of Family Rituals and Traditions 110

Reinforcing Positive Connections within the Family 112

In Conclusion 114

Chapter 6

Friendship: The Bonds That Sustain Us 116

The Evolution of Friendship in Adult Life 116

Qualities of Enduring Friendships... 118

Navigating Seasons of Change in Friendships..................... 120

The Impact of Social Media on Real Connections 122

Overcoming Betrayal and Disappointment in Friendships.... 125

How to Deepen Your Friendships 127

Creating a Circle of Trust: Choosing Friends Wisely 129

The Joy of Rekindling Old Friendships 131

Friendships Across Cultures: Learning and Growing Together
.... 133

Letting Go with Love: When Friendships Naturally End 135

In Conclusion.. 137

Chapter 7

Romantic Connections: Aligning Souls 138

Recognising a Soul Mate or Twin Flame................................ 140

Communication: The Heartbeat of Romance 143

Maintaining Individuality Within a Union.............................. 144

The Role of Intimacy and Vulnerability 147

Overcoming Challenges Together: Strengthening Your Bond 149

Healing Together: Working Through Past Traumas................ 151

The Importance of Shared Goals and Dreams 153

Rekindling the Spark: Keeping Love Alive............................. 155

When to Hold On and When to Let Go 157

In Conclusion.. 159

Chapter 8

The Workplace: Building Positive Professional Connections 161

The Importance of Emotional Intelligence at Work 161

Cultivating a Positive Work Environment.............................. 164

Setting Boundaries with Colleagues and Superiors 166

Recognising and Dealing with Workplace Energy Vampires .. 168

Building Collaborative Relationships 170

Nurturing Mentorships and Support Networks 172

Balancing Professionalism and Personal Connection 174

Leading with Empathy: The Role of Leadership in Workplace Energy 177

The Impact of Work-Life Balance on Professional Relationships 179

Transforming Conflict into Collaboration 181

In Conclusion 183

Chapter 9

Self-Connection: The Foundation of All Relationships 185

Understanding Your Inner Energy Landscape 185

The Importance of Self-Love and Self-Respect 187

Mindfulness: Being Present with Yourself 190

Managing Your Energy: Techniques and Practices 192

The Power of Solitude: Recharging Your Inner Battery 194

Aligning Your Actions with Your Values 196

The Role of Self-Reflection in Personal Growth 198

Overcoming Inner Critics: Building Inner Support 200

Cultivating Inner Peace: Practices for Emotional and Spiritual Well-being 202

Embracing Your Journey: The Path to Self-Discovery 204

Chapter 10

Impacting the World: The Ripple Effect of Positive Connections 208

The Concept of Social Responsibility in Relationships 208

Building Bridges: Overcoming Divides Through Understanding 210

The Role of Empathy in Societal Change 212

Volunteering and Community Service: Connecting Through Giving Back 215

The Global Tribe: Creating Connections Across Cultures 217

Acts of Kindness: Small Actions, Big Impact 219

The Power of Mentorship: Guiding the Next Generation........ 221

Advocacy and Social Change: Using Your Voice for Good..... 223

Acts of Generosity: Sharing Resources for a Greater Good ... 225

Paying It Forward: Creating a Cycle of Positive Impact 227

In Conclusion... 229

Final Word 231

Chapter 1

The Foundation of Connections

You are wired for connection. Your relationships, from acquaintances to lifelong companions, shape your emotional landscape and determine much of your well-being. In an ever-changing world, it can be easy to overlook the fundamental need for genuine connection. However, you crave it on a deep level, and when it is lacking, you sense the void acutely.

This chapter reveals the roots of human interaction. By understanding the core dynamics of connection and the emotional realities that govern you, you can set the stage for healthier, more fulfilling relationships. You do not simply stumble into meaningful bonds; you create them intentionally. Here, you will discover why emotional connectivity matters, how energy influences the bonds you form, and the ways empathy, boundaries, and self-awareness support genuine interaction.

You are not alone in wanting relationships that feed your soul. Emotions steer these connections, making you human. This chapter looks at how simple shifts, like setting positive intentions and respecting boundaries, can transform shallow interactions into profound, lifelong connections. You will also learn that self-awareness is a cornerstone for attracting those who enrich you rather than drain you. By the end, you will grasp that relationships can be nurtured into something powerful and uplifting. The insights within these pages are the foundation upon which you will build in subsequent chapters, each opening doors to deeper understanding.

The Importance of Emotional Connectivity

You thrive when you feel emotionally understood. Emotional connectivity involves sharing feelings, ideas, and stories in a way that resonates deeply. When you connect like this, the reward is immense: you feel heard and valued, and your relationships benefit from genuine exchange. This kind of bond, grounded in authentic emotion, acts as the glue that holds people together through good times and challenges alike. Emotional connectivity demands empathy. If you wish to strengthen your bonds, pay attention to the emotional cues someone sends out, whether through changes in voice or subtle facial expressions. Try your best to imagine what someone else is experiencing. For instance, if a friend feels overwhelmed by problems at work, move beyond polite responses. Ask questions, invite them to share details, and respond with genuine warmth. When you do, you convey that their emotions matter and that you are someone safe to turn to.

This depth of emotional exchange provides a protective cushion during difficulties. Stressful events, like job loss or family conflicts, can become more bearable when you have others who empathise and care. In these moments, your emotional bond provides reassurance. You are never meant to navigate burdens alone, and knowing that close confidants genuinely hear you reduces anxiety.

As you strengthen emotional connectivity, you will see the difference in how you communicate. Conversations become

The Foundation of Connections

less about passing information and more about sharing experiences. You become comfortable addressing delicate topics because you trust that the other person will respect your feelings. You also become more resilient because mutual care fosters an environment of understanding and support. For instance, if you are going through a difficult season, emotionally aware friends will notice changes in your mood. They may check in, lighten your load, or simply let you speak without interruption. In those moments, you feel the power of raw, heartfelt connection.

Emotional connectivity is not a one-sided endeavour. You must reveal your own feelings, as well. This openness can feel uneasy at first if you are used to being guarded. Yet it is through vulnerability that true emotional intimacy flourishes. You might worry about rejection, but you will often discover that revealing your fears and hopes deepens the bond. When you trust someone with your hidden side, you both embark on a shared journey of authenticity.

In essence, emotional connectivity lies at the core of your relationships. Without it, interactions can feel empty, leaving you searching for more. The emotional bridge you build with another allows for empathy, mutual respect, and true understanding. You become motivated to care sincerely for each other, standing together when life feels uncertain. As you develop this form of communication, you lay the groundwork for enriched connections that can stand the test of time. The chapters ahead will expand on these ideas, teaching you how to maintain emotional closeness even when life's pressures begin to mount.

Understanding Energy in Relationships

Connections

Everything in creation has its own energy, a concept that might sound abstract but becomes clearer once you notice how different people affect you. You may walk into a room and sense tension, only to learn later that two people had a heated argument. Alternatively, you might meet someone whose presence lifts your spirits without them saying much. These everyday experiences point to the vital role of energy in your relationships.

When you carry positive energy, rooted in gratitude, kindness, and sincerity, you draw in people who resonate with similar qualities. Conversely, carrying unresolved anger or constant pessimism can push others away, often unconsciously. Recognising this dynamic is key to cultivating meaningful relationships.

To harness positive energy, pay attention to your internal state. If you feel anxious, unsettled, or irritable, pause. Ask yourself what is causing these emotions. Is it stress from work or an unresolved personal issue? Perhaps it is something deeper, like disappointment from past experiences. Address these issues by engaging in practices that calm you, whether through prayer, breathing exercises, or journaling. Once you address your inner storm, you will find that social interactions become smoother.

Next, focus on how you present your energy to others. If you meet a friend while preoccupied with concerns, your tone and expressions may reflect that strain. Simply pausing to take a few deep breaths before you speak can help you centre yourself, which in turn creates a more welcoming atmosphere. When you prioritise kindness, you reduce tension in conversations, making them more open and constructive.

The Foundation of Connections

Boundaries are closely linked to your energy. Without them, you risk absorbing negativity from others or giving more than you can manage. You might have a relative who complains constantly, leaving you feeling drained. One approach is to acknowledge your own limits. That might mean limiting phone calls with them or gently steering conversations towards more balanced topics. Doing so protects your energy and prevents you from feeling overwhelmed. Once your energy is safeguarded, you can engage more empathetically.

It is worth noting that energy is not restricted to emotions. Physical and mental energy both come into play. If you neglect your body's needs, your overall energy can plummet. Lack of sleep, poor diet, or inadequate exercise may result in irritability or impatience, which inevitably affects those around you. By taking care of your health, you maintain a vibrant energy field that enhances communication and fosters deeper bonds.

Another significant point is collective energy. Think of a group of people who share a unified purpose, such as volunteers at a charitable event or sports fans cheering for a team. Their combined energy creates an atmosphere that can be electrifying and uplifting. The same is true for your personal circles. When you align with individuals who value kindness, truth, and respect, your collective energy amplifies. You support each other's goals, celebrate successes, and stand together during trials.

Your awareness of energy in your relationships is the first step in shaping them positively. When you handle your internal climate well and give out kindness and patience, you inspire those around you. You become a person they find comfort and encouragement in. Pay attention to your interactions this week. Notice times when you feel energised and times when you feel drained. The more attuned you are, the easier it becomes to balance and protect the energy you bring into your relationships.

Identifying Your Personal Energy Signature

Each person has a distinct energetic fingerprint, shaped by temperament, past experiences, and daily habits. You have qualities that radiate from you, sometimes unconsciously. Recognising these traits, or your personal energy signature, is essential when working toward healthier, more satisfying connections.

Start by reflecting on how you behave in various settings. Maybe you are warm, approachable, and quick to smile. Or perhaps you are more reserved, preferring to observe before engaging. Neither style is inherently better or worse, but awareness is crucial. When you understand how you usually act, you can choose to adjust when you realise you are not reflecting your best self.

Observe the patterns in your daily life. For instance, do you tend to be impatient? This impatience might manifest as interrupting people mid-sentence, rushing them to conclude their thoughts, or even feeling agitated in slow traffic. Such behavioural patterns highlight aspects of your energy signature that could repel the positive relationships you want. Identifying them is the first step to shifting toward a healthier approach.

You might also notice consistent emotional reactions. Do you respond to stress with anger, tears, or withdrawal? Once you determine the triggers behind these emotional

The Foundation of Connections

responses, you can begin to manage them instead of letting them dominate interactions. If a specific colleague's actions repeatedly upset you, question why. Are they genuinely overstepping your boundaries, or is something in your own experiences shaping that reaction? Sometimes, memories from past relationships or childhood experiences surface in surprising ways, casting a shadow over current connections.

It helps to ask friends or trusted family members what they see in you. You could say, "I am working on getting to know myself better. How do I usually come across when we are together?" Expect honesty, and listen. Their feedback, if given in good faith, can highlight blind spots. You might be surprised if your calm demeanour is interpreted as aloofness or if your humour sometimes gets misread as insensitivity. Critiques can be tough to hear, but they are invaluable for your growth.

You might also consider an internal check-in each morning or evening. Ask yourself how you are feeling physically, emotionally, and mentally. This quick self-scan is a simple way to catch early signs of imbalance. Perhaps you notice tension in your shoulders each morning, indicating lingering stress. By identifying this pattern, you can address it through stretching or other techniques before it escalates and influences your interactions.

Another valuable step is to consider your values. Your energy signature is partly shaped by what you hold as important, whether compassion, honesty, or loyalty. When your behaviour aligns with these values, you feel authentic; a mismatch triggers inner discord. For example, if you value honesty but often withhold true feelings, your relationships will lack depth, and your personal energy might feel stifled.

As you become more in tune with your personal energy signature, accept that improvement is a lifelong process. You might transform certain habits, only to discover new areas that need tweaking. This journey can be liberating. By gently shifting negative patterns into more positive expressions, you create space for relationships marked by openness, respect, and shared purpose. Paying attention to your energy signature is not about self-critique; it is about celebrating the positive aspects and making deliberate adjustments where needed. In doing so, you elevate the quality of all your connections.

The Psychology of Connection: Tribal Instincts in the Modern World

Humans have always relied on communal ties for survival. Historically, belonging to a tribe was a matter of life or death. These tribal instincts, which evolved for protection and cooperation, remain within you today, influencing how you connect with others. Yet the modern world, with its digital interactions and frequent relocations, complicates how you satisfy this innate longing.

Your ancestors formed tribes for shared benefits: collective hunting, child-rearing, and defence. Trust was essential, cemented through shared language and cultural rituals. Today, you do not typically hunt as a group or fend off physical threats together. But the drive to trust and be trusted remains potent. You still gravitate toward people who feel familiar or safe. That is why you often form friendship groups around mutual interests, shared backgrounds, or like-minded values.

In today's environment, forging a sense of tribe can be both simpler and more complex. Technology helps you meet like-

The Foundation of Connections

minded individuals from anywhere. However, superficial digital exchanges can create hollow forms of kinship. You might have hundreds of online "friends," yet still crave genuine bonds. The key is ensuring you move beyond surface-level interactions into deeper emotional territory. If you find an online group with similar pursuits, reach out in a more personal way. Ask genuine questions, share experiences, and be open to reciprocating. True tribal bonds rely on more than quick likes or fleeting chats.

Tribal instincts can also lead to exclusion if you become closed off to those who do not share your views. This primal tendency to see outsiders as threats can harm modern relationships. Consider the divisive climate online, where individuals are quick to judge those on the "other side." Understanding your instinct to remain loyal to your in-group can help you remain courteous during disagreements. Focus on universal human traits, such as the desire for happiness and safety, to avoid creating unnecessary barriers.

Family ties often highlight tribal instincts, as they are often your first sense of community. Extended family gatherings can rekindle the sense of unity that is rooted in shared heritage. However, tension can arise when personal values conflict with family norms. Reflect on how to balance loyalty with self-expression. Sometimes, establishing healthy boundaries while maintaining respect is key to preserving peace within the family unit, as this is still your tribe.

Workplaces also draw upon tribal impulses. Teams often function at their best when members feel an "us" mentality, motivating each person to exceed expectations. When you are part of a strong team, you share in collective victories, forging a sense of camaraderie. Conflicts do appear, but you can harness empathy, open communication, and conflict-resolution strategies. Tapping into your tribal instincts productively fosters unity and drives shared achievements.

Outside personal and professional circles, you can see the tribal instinct in how people champion sports teams or political movements. These alignments create a powerful sense of belonging. While that unity can be uplifting, be mindful of not losing your individuality or scorning those who choose differently. A balanced perspective recognises how your primal drive to belong shapes your loyalty and interactions. Appreciating this aspect of human psychology encourages you to be more compassionate and patient with yourself and others.

Thus, your tribal nature is alive and well, albeit in modern contexts. Embrace it by seeking out fulfilling, reciprocal communities while staying aware of the possibility of groupthink or exclusivity. When channelled wisely, your instinct to band together can build strong networks, fostering collaboration and mutual support. The future of human connection depends on how you respond to these ancestral drives in a rapidly evolving social landscape.

The Spectrum of Social Bonds: From Acquaintances to Soulmates

Your social life is not binary. It is a wide-ranging tapestry of relationships (avoiding the restricted word), each fulfilling a different need in your life. Acquaintances, for instance, may meet your desire for light, casual interaction. You might chat about weather or weekend plans. These connections can be pleasant but lack emotional depth. On the other side of the spectrum lie soulmates, individuals who seem to resonate with your core essence. They understand you, sometimes without many words, and share an unshakable bond.

Acquaintances are neither insignificant nor superficial by default. They can be stepping stones to deeper connections. Many solid friendships start casually, beginning with small talk that eventually blossoms into trust. The same is true of your professional circle. A colleague you speak to while grabbing a coffee could one day become a close friend if you find shared interests or values that spark deeper conversations.

Between casual acquaintances and soulmates are various levels of closeness: friendly neighbours, old school friends you see sporadically, workmates you get on with, and deeper, supportive friends you confide in regularly. Each relationship has its purpose, adding colour and variety to your social life. Knowing the role each bond plays allows you to manage expectations. For example, you would not confide your deepest secrets to someone you only see on social occasions. By being aware of these distinctions, you can also avoid feeling disappointed when certain interactions lack the intimacy you might crave.

At the soulmate end of the spectrum, you find relationships enriched by profound emotional and sometimes spiritual connection. You may not share all the same beliefs or interests, but there is an unspoken understanding. These individuals see your strengths and flaws and appreciate you in totality. They have your back. Your interactions with them feel energising, as though you are both aligned. It is also important to note that the term "soulmate" is not always limited to romantic contexts; you can experience a similarly deep bond with a close friend. These relationships might develop over time or appear unexpectedly, but they often serve as a cornerstone in your emotional life.

Recognising where each relationship falls on this spectrum helps you manage your emotional investment. If you treat acquaintances as potential best friends without the necessary mutual emotional trust, you may strain the bond. Alternatively, if you treat a close friend with the same casual nature as an acquaintance, you risk neglecting a relationship that could become truly meaningful. Strive for balance and clarity, both for your sake and for those around you.

It is worth noting that your connections can shift over time. Old friends might drift apart due to new life circumstances, and acquaintances might grow into dear friends as you find fresh common ground. Be open to these evolutions. Stay attentive to your own feelings and your friends' signals. Communication is key in any dynamic, letting you navigate changes with honesty and respect.

Ultimately, your social bonds form a community, each link vital in some capacity. Even the person you exchange quick pleasantries with can play a role in shaping your mood and day. Embrace the variety of connections in your life, acknowledging that each can grow and deepen given the right circumstances. By understanding the spectrum of relationships, you grant yourself the freedom to nurture them according to their natural depth, all while creating a richer, more gratifying social life.

The Role of Empathy in Building Strong Connections

Empathy is the bridge that allows you to step into another person's emotional space. You might know how painful heartbreak is or how fulfilling success can feel, yet empathy

The Foundation of Connections

transforms these abstract understandings into genuine compassion. It is essential for forging the robust relationships you crave because it speaks the universal language of the heart: I see you. I acknowledge your emotions.

Being empathetic does not require that you solve someone's issues. Instead, your aim is to understand them. When a friend reveals worries about a health crisis, do not rush to provide cures. Pause and truly listen. Show you understand their fear or frustration. This small act of feeling with them can alleviate their isolation more than any hasty solution. Likewise, in a professional environment, empathising with a co-worker under deadline stress might encourage you to offer help or simply say, "I understand how tough that is," bridging a gap that keeps tensions from escalating.

A hurdle for empathy arises when you disagree with someone's viewpoint or choices. Though it is easy to empathise when you share feelings, the real test is empathising with a stance that counters your own beliefs. Practising empathy here means focusing on the person's emotional experience rather than their conclusion. You might never agree with a friend's political stance, but you can empathise with their fears or hopes that fuel that perspective. This approach often softens hostilities, creating a space where genuine conversation can thrive.

Empathy should not be confused with pity. Pity can feel distancing because it tends to place you in a superior position, looking down on someone else's pain. Genuine empathy is about understanding from a level ground. You stand beside them in spirit, showing them they are not alone. This solidarity fosters trust and can mend fractures in your relationships. In a family context, if a sibling feels overlooked, empathising with their position can ease sibling rivalry. You may not fully agree with their viewpoint, but your willingness to see how they feel can be healing.

Empathy is also beneficial to your own well-being. When you show sincere empathy, your body often releases positive neurochemicals that help you feel more connected and less stressed. At the same time, empathy encourages a more open mindset. You step out of your isolated bubble and engage with the wide tapestry (avoiding restricted word) of human experience. This broadening perspective can inspire personal growth, showing you how resilient people can be when faced with life's complexities.

Developing deeper empathy starts with active listening. Practice leaning in, making eye contact, and withholding judgment. Reflect on what you hear. If a friend confides feelings of loneliness, respond gently with phrases like, "That must be difficult," or "I can sense how much this weighs on you." These validations affirm that you acknowledge their emotions. When appropriate, ask questions that help them elaborate, letting them know you genuinely want to understand.

Moreover, keep in mind that empathy balances with boundaries. If you internalise everyone's struggles, you risk draining your own emotional reserves. By recognising this, you will sense when to step back and recharge. This also reminds you that empathy is not about carrying another's burdens but offering a caring presence. In nurturing empathy, you become a beacon of support, forging connections built on mutual understanding. Embrace this practice, and watch as it enriches not only your relationships but also your perspective on life.

Setting Boundaries: The Balance Between Giving and Receiving

Healthy relationships do not require endless self-sacrifice. You may believe that demonstrating your loyalty means always saying yes, offering unceasing support without regard for your energy. In reality, boundaries are essential for relationships that truly flourish. They safeguard your well-being and promote respect. If you often feel depleted or resentful after interactions, it is likely your boundaries need reevaluation.

Boundaries define how much you can give before your emotional and physical resources run low. They help you clarify what is acceptable to you, preventing potential mistreatment or misinterpretations. People who respect your boundaries are more likely to become trusted companions, acknowledging you are not a means to an end but a person with valid needs. On the other hand, those who constantly ignore your boundaries may cause friction in your life.

Boundaries can be psychological, such as the emotional topics you are willing (or unwilling) to discuss, or physical, like personal space and time management. If you have a friend who calls late every night, bringing negativity that disrupts your sleep, a boundary might mean letting them know you will not pick up calls after a certain hour. Doing so does not mean you do not care about their troubles. Rather, it shows respect for your own well-being, ensuring you can be fully present and supportive when you choose to engage.

Connections

One challenge is learning to articulate boundaries calmly, without guilt or aggression. Start by making clear, concise statements: "I appreciate your concern, but I need some alone time this weekend," or "I hear your viewpoint, but I am not comfortable discussing that topic." Practice these statements in your mind so you can deliver them gently yet firmly. Standing your ground might feel awkward if you are unaccustomed to it, but it is an expression of self-respect. Observing how people respond can be an excellent indicator of whether they value you beyond what you can do for them.

A lack of boundaries can also appear at work. You might consistently accept additional tasks, hoping to please your boss or colleagues, eventually leading to exhaustion. Learning to say no politely when you are near capacity is a skill. You might say, "I have a full workload at the moment; is it possible to revisit this later?" or "I am happy to help, but can we adjust the deadline?" By setting these professional boundaries, you preserve your energy and maintain a sense of balance that ultimately enhances performance.

Boundaries are not static; they can evolve as you grow. What you find acceptable in your 20s might shift by your 40s as life circumstances change. That is natural. Regularly reassess whether your boundaries still serve you. If you find yourself consistently uncomfortable in certain relationships, it may be that your boundaries need adjustment. Perhaps you have become more discerning about where you invest emotional energy, or your job demands a different distribution of time.

Finally, remember that boundaries also apply to what you expect from others. You might decide not to overstep lines, such as calling someone incessantly or demanding immediate replies to messages. Respect for others' privacy

The Foundation of Connections

and emotional states fosters reciprocal respect. Setting boundaries, then, is not merely about self-preservation; it is about mutual regard. When you cultivate that healthy equilibrium, you create space for deeper and more genuine connections.

The Science of Vibrations: How We Attract and Repel

Beneath the everyday complexities of human interaction lies a more subtle force often described as vibrations. You see these vibrations in moments where certain people brighten a room upon arrival, while others dampen the mood. These experiences hint at an unseen but potent influence that shapes how people respond to you and how you respond to them.

Your vibrational frequency correlates to your emotional states and thought patterns. Picture two radios tuned to different frequencies. They cannot communicate unless they align on the same wavelength. Humans operate similarly. When your frequency resonates with another's, you feel immediate rapport. This can manifest as finishing each other's sentences, feeling comfortable sharing personal stories, or simply sensing an unspoken bond.

What affects these frequencies? A great deal depends on your mindset. Positive feelings like optimism and gratitude usually elevate your vibrational level, making your presence more welcoming. Conversely, chronic negativity can create a lower, denser vibration, repelling those who prefer more uplifting surroundings. People often describe such individuals as having "bad vibes."

You have more control over your frequency than you might think. Start with awareness. Notice how you feel after

Connections

engaging with certain activities. Do you feel lighter or heavier after watching particular news segments or scrolling through negative comment sections? If you notice your mood dipping, shift your focus toward something uplifting. Perhaps a walk, uplifting music, or reading an inspirational text. You are training yourself to self-regulate, which helps maintain a balanced frequency.

A practical exercise involves visualisation. Before you begin your day or enter an important meeting, pause. Breathe slowly and visualise a bright, calm aura encircling you. This simple mental exercise can help you project a stable, uplifting energy. Though it might seem too simple, many find such mental rehearsals effective for reducing anxiety and fostering a positive mood.

On the other side, watch out for patterns that drag you down. If you often share in gossip or cynicism, your frequency can drop, which might deter the positive individuals you want in your life. Shift your communication style. Use uplifting language and acknowledge the good in situations whenever possible. Over time, you will notice that your circle shifts, attracting those who appreciate positivity.

Being mindful of your vibrational output also extends to the way you handle emotional turmoil. When sadness or stress arises, address it rather than bury it. Speak with a trusted friend or seek a constructive outlet, like writing or physical activity. By confronting and processing heavy emotions, you prevent them from solidifying into a permanent low vibration.

Relationships come alive when both parties share higher, compatible frequencies. Conversations flow smoothly, support is mutual, and even disagreements transform into respectful dialogues rather than heated quarrels. Achieving

The Foundation of Connections

this does not imply never experiencing negative emotions. Life includes stress, heartbreak, and anger, which are normal. Rather, it is about how swiftly you identify and regulate those emotions. The quicker you address and release them, the more consistently you remain in a higher state, capable of nurturing healthy connections.

Understanding vibrations is not a cure-all but an invaluable tool for navigating social and emotional landscapes. By consciously lifting your own frequency, you not only invite warmth and authenticity in others but also contribute to a more harmonious environment. Though you cannot alter someone else's vibrations directly, you can adjust your own. Doing that alone can be enough to foster an atmosphere where positivity and mutual respect thrive.

Cultivating Self-Awareness to Enhance Connectivity

Your capacity to connect with others increases dramatically when you know yourself well. Self-awareness is more than identifying favourite foods or music tastes. It involves recognising emotional triggers, understanding how you react under pressure, and being conscious of your personal needs. Once you gain clarity on these internal aspects, you become more attuned to what drives you and how you impact those around you.

To start, examine your emotional triggers. Think about times you lost your temper or felt unexpectedly hurt. What sparked those feelings? Perhaps certain topics, such as finances or personal criticisms, set you off. By identifying these triggers, you gain the power to approach these subjects more calmly next time. Maybe you used to react defensively when faced with a specific critique from a spouse. Recognising this pattern allows you to pause before replying, making a deliberate choice rather than firing back impulsively.

Next, explore how you handle stress. Everyone faces challenging moments, but responses vary greatly. Some bury themselves in work, others withdraw socially, and still others overindulge in comfort activities, like binge-watching or over-snacking. If you detect unhelpful coping strategies, begin replacing them with healthier alternatives. Maybe you can take a short walk or talk to a supportive friend. By practising self-awareness, you become mindful of these behavioural shifts and can address them before they erode your relationships.

Another cornerstone is introspection. Periodically reflect on your interactions during a typical day. Are you speaking kindly, or do you rush to judge? Do you fully listen, or do you mentally compose your response while someone else is talking? You can catch habits that undermine authentic connection. This self-check is not about chastising yourself; it is about noticing and gently adjusting. Over time, such consistent reflection refines your social skills.

Understanding your strengths and limitations is also key. If you are a natural listener but shy about speaking up, you might find yourself supporting others yet rarely sharing your perspective. Recognise this tendency. In some relationships, you may need to push beyond your comfort zone to ensure balance. By contrast, if you love being in the spotlight, watch that you do not overshadow quieter friends. Self-awareness helps you modulate so everyone feels valued.

Journaling is an excellent tool for building self-awareness. Take a few minutes daily or weekly to note significant emotional highs or lows. Write about how you responded and whether you could have handled it differently. This written record can help spot patterns, highlighting triggers and revealing growth opportunities. It also offers a safe space to clarify your thoughts.

Additionally, meaningful conversations with people you trust can reveal blind spots. Ask a close friend or family member how you come across in groups. Their perspective might unveil habits you do not notice, such as interrupting or appearing disinterested. While such feedback can sting, it also presents a valuable chance for self-improvement. Approach these insights with an open heart, realising they are given to help, not to humiliate.

Ultimately, self-awareness is a catalyst for deeper connections because it underpins authenticity. You cannot be sincerely present for others if you are not present in yourself. When you know your triggers, your coping style, your emotional responses, and your relational strengths, you move through social encounters with greater confidence and sincerity. This authentic energy resonates. People sense that you are genuine, encouraging them to respond in kind. Embrace self-awareness as your ally; it refines the way you interact and paves a smoother path for the meaningful bonds you want.

The Power of Intention in Relationships

In a world brimming with distractions, the difference between a thriving relationship and a stagnant one often lies in intentionality. When you set clear intentions, you infuse purpose and direction into your interactions. An intention is like a mental compass guiding you toward the quality of connection you desire. It keeps you focused on what matters most: trust, respect, empathy, or any value you hold dear.

Intentional relationships do not just happen. If you want more meaningful conversations, set the tone by giving your full attention, minimising phone usage, and asking thoughtful questions. If you seek deeper emotional intimacy, communicate your feelings openly and encourage the other person to share as well. By stating, "I aim to be more patient today," or "I will be kinder and more supportive," you set a benchmark for your behaviour. You then strive to live up to it, especially when challenges arise.

An essential element of intention is consistency. Imagine saying you will be punctual for meetings as a sign of respect, only to arrive late half the time. The mismatch between declared intention and behaviour undermines trust. On the other hand, consistently aligned actions strengthen your credibility and your relationships. People come to rely on you because they see you walk your talk.

You can apply intention in simple, everyday ways. Before meeting someone, spend a few seconds mentally affirming what you hope to bring to the conversation. Maybe you want to be a comforting presence to a friend who is upset. Or, if you are part of a team at work, you might aim to be the voice of optimism during a tough project. These mini-affirmations prime your mindset, making you more likely to act in accordance with your goal. Over time, these intentions become a habit, shaping how you engage with the world.

When disagreements surface, as they inevitably do, a focus on intention can turn confrontation into collaboration. Instead of entering an argument with the aim of being right, decide your goal is mutual understanding. You might say, "I

The Foundation of Connections

want us both to feel heard and respected." This helps keep your emotions in check because you remember the higher purpose behind the conversation. You are not out to score points; you are there to connect meaningfully and solve issues.

Intentions also help you reflect more accurately on your daily experiences. If you notice conflict arising regularly with a particular family member, question whether your underlying intention has become to protect yourself or prove a point rather than to support the relationship. This introspection can highlight how your focus may have shifted from building bridges to guarding your ego. Simply resetting your intention can make a big difference in how you communicate.

Far from being forced positivity, intention is about alignment. It does not mean ignoring genuine emotions, like anger or hurt, but guiding those emotions constructively. You can say, "I feel upset, but I also want to maintain respect." This approach acknowledges reality while still upholding your personal values. By staying centred on that intention, you practice self-control, which often leads to more harmonious resolutions.

In sum, intention forms the hidden bedrock of successful, nurturing relationships. Whether in small gestures or major life decisions, it roots you in purposeful, honourable action. People can sense your sincerity, which fosters trust and collaboration. By consciously choosing what you aim to bring to each relationship, you help shape that bond's depth and character. You transform the routine of daily interaction into something imbued with care, kindness, and clarity of purpose.

In Conclusion

You have taken your first steps into understanding the bedrock of all connections: emotional connectivity, energetic awareness, and mindful intention. By nurturing these elements, you set yourself up for richer, more rewarding relationships. From the simple act of empathising to the deeper challenge of managing your personal energy field, you now see how deliberate effort can strengthen every bond in your life.

In the chapters ahead, you will dive deeper into specifics: from discovering uplifting people, warding off those who drain you, and forging your supportive tribe to cultivating the love and friendship that keep you grounded. The foundation you have laid here is crucial. You will continue to build upon it, applying the tools of empathy, self-awareness, and intention. These key insights remain at the heart of every chapter to come, guiding you toward ever more meaningful connections.

Chapter 2

Energy Givers: The Source of Light

This chapter celebrates the uplifting souls in your life. Energy Givers, as you will soon explore, brighten conversations, motivate you to grow, and encourage your dreams. Their presence is a steady current of positivity, renewing your faith in life and in yourself. You will learn to identify, attract, and nurture bonds with these generous-spirited individuals. With them around, your journey becomes lighter, more hopeful, and less plagued by negativity.

It is not that Energy Givers are flawless or never have challenges. Rather, they maintain an energy that promotes hope, showing you that difficulties need not consume you. This chapter will examine their characteristics, reveal how they impact your life, and teach you ways to ensure these relationships remain reciprocal and respectful. Because a strong community is essential to a fulfilling life, you will learn to be intentional in seeking out such people and in being one yourself. Let us begin by studying the traits that define these uplifting figures and discovering how they can shape your world.

Characteristics of Energy Givers

Energy Givers possess attributes that make them stand out in any crowd. You may notice that they have a calm demeanour, an active listening style, and a knack for injecting positivity even when the mood is sombre. One telltale sign is their sense of empathy. These individuals genuinely care about what you have to say, asking purposeful questions that demonstrate real interest. It is not that they never talk about themselves, but they remain genuinely curious about you, as well.

Another key characteristic is consistency. Many people might offer a quick compliment, but an Energy Giver consistently uplifts those around them without expecting returns. Perhaps they leave you thoughtful notes when you are having a tough day or remember small details from a conversation weeks ago. Their consistent kindness builds trust. You feel secure that their warmth is not a temporary facade.

Despite their supportive nature, Energy Givers are not pushovers. They hold a strong sense of self and maintain clear boundaries. This might sound surprising, but it is precisely because they understand the importance of protecting their own well-being. By taking care of themselves, they can more authentically offer positivity. Consequently, an Energy Giver will not let others mistreat them. They also do not just agree to keep the peace. Instead, they calmly express their perspectives, show empathy, and foster mutual respect.

Many Energy Givers exhibit a problem-solving orientation. Rather than dwelling on complaints, they gravitate toward looking for solutions or focusing on the silver lining. This trait does not make them naive. They understand life's weighty aspects, yet they choose to channel their energy into constructive thinking. If you confide in one about a personal dilemma, they will empathise but also gently encourage you to see options you might have overlooked.

Energy Givers: The Source of Light

Energy Givers often practice gratitude, one of the most potent forces for lifting mood. They keep life's blessings in mind, whether it is a warm home or a supportive circle of friends. This gratitude seeps into their relationships, showing up as compliments, supportive remarks, or gestures of appreciation. Their sense of thankfulness is contagious, reminding you to notice the goodness in your own life. Over time, you might feel more inspired around them, realising that there is much to savour every day.

Curiosity is another hallmark. Because they see life as an ongoing learning experience, they approach situations with open-mindedness. This curiosity extends to people, driving them to listen rather than judge. If you talk about a goal that others dismiss as unrealistic, they are more likely to ask how you plan to achieve it. Their inquisitive nature can breathe life into your aspirations, guiding you to refine them instead of discarding them in discouragement.

Finally, Energy Givers see the best in others. They recognise flaws but choose to focus on potential, and their faith in your abilities can be a huge motivator when you doubt yourself. This does not mean they ignore reality, but they emphasise hope and possibility. As a result, their presence is akin to a steady light, illuminating paths you may not have noticed. Once you observe these characteristics, you begin to see the difference between fleeting positivity and a truly uplifting presence that remains vibrant, even when external circumstances are tough.

The Impact of Positive Energy on Your Life

Positive energy is transformative. It radiates beyond the boundaries of any single relationship, affecting how you perceive yourself and the world. When you spend time with people who emit this brightness, you often experience a cascade of benefits: improved mood, heightened creativity, and deeper resilience. It is not mere coincidence that your best ideas may surface after a fulfilling conversation with an uplifting friend. The synergy of positivity encourages your mind to be more open and adventurous.

Emotionally, positive energy can alleviate stress and anxiety. Have you noticed how your posture changes around those who make you feel safe and valued? Shoulders loosen, breathing slows, and you speak more freely. This ease allows you to articulate feelings and ideas you might otherwise bury. In turn, you enjoy healthier emotional expression, preventing resentment or bitterness from festering.

Socially, positivity fuels connection. After all, you gravitate towards individuals who affirm your worth rather than those who constantly criticise. When you are nurtured in an encouraging environment, you become more willing to reach out and expand your network. You might attend more events, try new activities, or connect with friends-of-friends, confident in your ability to form meaningful bonds. Over time, this fosters a supportive community that stands by you, amplifying the benefits of positivity.

Positive energy also has a significant effect on physical well-being. Chronic negativity can elevate stress hormones, leading to health issues. By contrast, consistent positivity tends to lower stress-related ailments. Of course, life can still be messy, and positivity is not a magical shield, but an optimistic mindset bolstered by uplifting relationships can encourage healthier choices. Maybe you exercise more, cook nutritious meals, or sleep better simply because you

Energy Givers: The Source of Light

feel motivated and cared for. This synergy of better self-care and good emotional health further strengthens your ability to handle adversity.

One fascinating aspect is how positivity in one area seeps into another. Say you feel particularly energised after a heartening talk with a close friend. You might direct this uplift into your work, tackling tasks with newfound creativity and efficiency. This success at work then boosts your confidence, further improving your personal interactions. In this way, positive energy acts like a feedback loop, each positive occurrence fuelling another.

But positivity should not be confused with denying negative realities. Energy Givers often demonstrate a balanced outlook. They acknowledge hardships but channel their focus toward what can be done. Their approach is more about resilience than naive optimism. They remind you that pain is part of life but does not define it. This perspective fosters mental fortitude, making you less likely to crumble under stress. Instead, you gather strength to adapt and overcome.

In daily life, small positive gestures can accumulate. An encouraging text message, an unexpected compliment, or a friendly check-in all contribute to a shared atmosphere that keeps you buoyant. These small acts might not erase life's obstacles, but they do provide consistent rays of hope. Over time, you learn that positivity is a resource you can cultivate, drawing upon it to remain steady through the storm. Ultimately, you realise it is not only your personal circle that benefits; your sunny spirit can ripple outwards, inspiring others to approach life with more optimism and grace.

How to Attract and Recognise Energy Givers

Attracting Energy Givers begins with reflecting on your own outlook. Before you identify them in your surroundings, ask yourself: Do I exude positivity or negativity? Your disposition often signals to potential Energy Givers whether you align with their uplifting presence. If your conversations are dominated by criticism or complaints, Energy Givers might distance themselves, not wanting their vibrancy diluted.

A helpful exercise is to notice your own language patterns. How frequently do you voice appreciation or highlight solutions as opposed to fixating on problems? If you find negativity creeping into your daily speech, challenge it with balanced or encouraging phrases. For example, switch statements like "Everything is going wrong" to "I am facing challenges, but I know there is a path forward." Over time, this shift can make a real difference, inviting people who resonate with that can-do spirit.

Recognising Energy Givers when you see them is another step. Typically, you feel uplifted after speaking to them, as though a weight has been lifted from your shoulders. They greet you warmly, maintain interested eye contact, and appear genuinely curious about your day. They do not shy from constructive dialogues but shy away from gossip or excessive blame. If you express frustration, they may listen intently and offer a word of encouragement or a practical step to alleviate stress.

Observe how these individuals handle group dynamics. If someone is being overshadowed or spoken over, Energy Givers tend to address or redirect focus kindly, making sure everyone feels included. They also stand out in crisis, as they keep calm, assessing how to help or what advice might be

Energy Givers: The Source of Light

needed, rather than spiralling into panic. When you notice such traits, you have likely identified an Energy Giver.

Finding new Energy Givers requires actively pursuing positivity in your environment. Consider joining groups or clubs where constructive conversation is the norm, such as fitness communities, book clubs, or volunteer organisations. Positive environments often attract warm-hearted individuals. Look for community gatherings dedicated to shared hobbies or local charities. People who give their time freely often have a natural inclination towards uplifting others.

Do not underestimate online platforms, either. Niche groups dedicated to art, cooking, or other interests can serve as spaces where positivity thrives. While you must remain cautious about the superficial nature of online interactions, meaningful connections do exist there. Engaging in constructive online discussions with courtesy and empathy can lead you to Energy Givers from around the globe, broadening your perspective.

Finally, it is not enough to find these people; you must also nurture these connections. If you meet someone who genuinely lightens your spirit, show gratitude. Send a note expressing appreciation for their insight or positivity. Offer your support in return. Reciprocity cements these relationships and signals to them that you value what they bring to your life. Energy Givers are not there to carry you indefinitely; the relationship must remain balanced, with mutual respect and care. By doing your part in upholding positivity, you create a welcoming environment that keeps these radiant souls in your circle.

Connections

Nurturing Relationships with Energy Givers

Once you have identified Energy Givers, the real work is maintaining and deepening those connections. These relationships flourish when both parties reciprocate. Though Energy Givers naturally share optimism and support, they also benefit from receiving kindness, appreciation, and empathy. Think of this bond as a plant that thrives when both sun and water are consistently provided.

Aim to cultivate a space of mutual uplift. Begin by showing genuine gratitude. Energy Givers often give freely, without expecting praise, but a heartfelt "Thank you, your help meant a lot," or "I really value your insight," can make a difference. Such acknowledgements feed the synergy that sustains healthy bonds. It reminds them that their supportive nature is noticed and cherished, which in turn encourages them to keep radiating positivity.

Active listening is another cornerstone. Energy Givers might not always broadcast their troubles, but that does not mean they never face hardship. If you sense they are overwhelmed or less vibrant than usual, reach out. Ask questions. Lend a compassionate ear. Being aware of their needs shows that the relationship is not one-sided. You shift from being merely a beneficiary to a caring companion who can return the warmth they offer.

As the relationship evolves, consider shared experiences. Spend time doing activities that inspire both of you, such as attending uplifting seminars, enjoying nature walks, or collaborating on creative projects. Joint participation in positive endeavours amplifies the beneficial energy you both bring, often solidifying the connection further. In such shared environments, you reinforce each other's strengths, while

Energy Givers: The Source of Light

building a reservoir of joyful memories to draw upon during tough times.

Boundaries also play a role. While Energy Givers hold a wellspring of positivity, they can become overwhelmed if you depend on them constantly. Be mindful not to treat them as an endless supply of emotional support. Engage in open communication to ensure they feel comfortable. If you are going through a challenging season, that is understandable, but check in to confirm you are not burdening them unnecessarily. Respecting their needs preserves a harmonious balance.

Conflict does arise in any relationship, even with someone generally uplifting. If disagreements crop up, address them openly yet compassionately. Energy Givers typically respond well to calm, constructive dialogue. If they sense your willingness to find common ground, they will likely reciprocate. Work through misunderstandings by focusing on solutions rather than rehashing the problem. This approach helps you both maintain the positive energy that underpins your bond.

A final element is personal growth. Energy Givers are often on a path of self-improvement, and they appreciate friends who share that outlook. Consider discussing personal goals or challenges. Cheer each other on. This mutual commitment to bettering yourselves fosters an environment where all parties feel motivated. Whether you set weekly goals to read more, adopt healthier habits, or focus on gratitude, having supportive friends by your side greatly multiplies your chances of success.

By consistently applying these steps, you create a dynamic bond with Energy Givers. The trust strengthens, the positivity deepens, and each interaction becomes a bright spot in your day. Remember, it is not about being perpetually cheerful. It is about offering warmth and compassion consistently, so that even in dark moments, your shared spirit illuminates the path forward.

The Role of Gratitude in Relationships with Energy Givers

Gratitude is a linchpin in fostering and sustaining relationships with Energy Givers. These individuals offer their warmth and encouragement freely, but it is your acknowledgment of their support that creates a meaningful cycle of reciprocity. Think of gratitude as the gentle glue that binds you and another, reinforcing the mutual goodwill that brought you together in the first place.

When you express gratitude, you remind the Energy Giver that their effort matters. They may already sense satisfaction from uplifting others, but hearing a sincere "I appreciate you" can revitalise their motivation. Sometimes, you can become so comfortable receiving their support that you overlook acknowledging it. By regularly voicing thankfulness, you keep the relationship balanced and affirm that you are aware of their kindness.

Such expressions of gratitude do not need to be grand or formal. Simple, heartfelt gestures work wonders. A quick message saying, "Thank you for your encouraging words earlier; they really helped me see things differently," can make their day. You could also write a short note or give them something small but meaningful, like a written card or a hand-crafted token of appreciation. The real value lies in the sentiment. These tokens confirm that you truly see their efforts.

Energy Givers: The Source of Light

Moreover, gratitude fosters a healthier internal state for you, too. Research shows that adopting a thankful mindset can reduce stress, foster optimism, and even improve sleep. When you take a moment to reflect on how an Energy Giver has enriched your day, you cultivate a spirit of appreciation. This sense of gratitude colours your perspective, making you more open and positive, which in turn helps you deepen your bond with that person. They become even more inclined to share their uplifting energy when they sense it is genuinely received and treasured.

There is also an interpersonal ripple effect. Gratitude often prompts more giving, not just from the Energy Giver, but from you as well. Recognising what you have received can inspire you to pass kindness on, either back to them or to another person in your circle. This cycle of giving and receiving nurtures a supportive network that raises the collective positivity. If your friend is always offering their ear, perhaps you pay it forward by sharing an inspiring book or helping a neighbour with errands. These actions keep the momentum of positivity alive.

Another angle of gratitude is the humility it brings. By being thankful, you acknowledge you do not have to handle life alone. Pride can sometimes hinder you from fully embracing and crediting the assistance you receive. Gratitude, on the other hand, humbly admits, "I am grateful for your role in my journey," which fosters genuine closeness and understanding. It removes any walls of self-sufficiency that might block deeper connection.

In cultivating a lifestyle of gratitude, you may find the practice extends beyond your relationship with Energy Givers. You start noticing the good in everyday experiences, from a morning cup of tea to a meaningful conversation with a colleague. As you develop this habit, your interactions become more heartfelt and your sense of well-being grows. Eventually, your resonance might transform you into an Energy Giver for someone else, continuing the chain reaction of positivity. Such is the power of gratitude in your relationships, it uplifts, unites, and keeps the flame of kindness burning bright.

Creating a Supportive and Uplifting Community

Building a community that uplifts you is a purposeful endeavour. You may find yourself surrounded by acquaintances who do not necessarily drag you down but do not contribute positivity either. Alternatively, you might have a small circle of extremely supportive friends but wish for a broader group of like-minded folks. Creating a supportive network involves both deliberate outreach and a commitment to nurturing the relationships that form around you.

Start by clarifying the atmosphere you hope to cultivate. Do you want friends with whom you can share personal goals and hold each other accountable? Or are you seeking a lighter, more socially oriented circle that emphasises relaxation and shared hobbies? Once you establish your priority, you can direct your energy into spaces likely to yield those connections. For instance, if you crave deeper spiritual or emotional exchanges, you might search for seminars, retreats, or interest groups that focus on self-development. If you prefer a sociable environment, explore local clubs, sports teams, or social meetups that emphasise camaraderie.

Energy Givers: The Source of Light

As you expand your circle, stay open-minded. Not everyone you meet in these settings will become a close friend. However, each event or gathering could spark a connection that enriches your life. You might meet an artist who becomes a creative collaborator, or a fellow parent whose experiences align with yours, allowing you to swap advice. By approaching each social interaction with an attitude of curiosity, you keep the door open for unexpected connections.

Fostering this community also depends on consistency. A single meeting is seldom enough to establish trust. Commit to regular meetups, weekly or monthly, so you can observe each other's growth and share ongoing experiences. For example, if you join a local volunteer group, turn up consistently. Steady participation indicates you are reliable, which encourages others to open up to you. Over time, you will establish a comfort zone within that collective.

Respect the diversity within your community. People bring different personalities, backgrounds, and talents. Some might be outgoing, others more reserved. Learn how to interact well with each type. For example, the quieter members may shine in smaller group discussions, while the more extroverted might thrive in bigger gatherings. By acknowledging these differences, you create an inclusive environment. Everyone feels seen and valued, strengthening the mutual support system.

Mutual aid is crucial. You might share job leads, discuss experiences that help each other navigate life's challenges, or coordinate assistance during personal hardships. Maybe you excel at organising events, and another friend is great at cooking. By pooling your strengths, the group becomes a network that fortifies every member's daily life. In this environment, you all evolve, gaining skills, knowledge, and emotional support. Everyone's successes feel collectively shared, while burdens become lighter when approached together.

Of course, fostering this sense of community calls for a dash of patience. People's schedules conflict, priorities change, and you might face the occasional misunderstanding. If a dispute arises, handle it with empathy. Open communication is the linchpin that resolves tensions before they fracture the group. Whether the group is small or large, consistency in respectful dialogue ensures it remains cohesive.

Ultimately, building an uplifting community can be among the most rewarding investments you make. As the circle grows, you will find yourself buoyed by warmth and encouragement, often offering the same in return. This supportive network weaves into the broader fabric of your life, offering security and joy that extends far beyond casual social interaction. In synergy, you lift each other higher, embodying the essence of what it means to share positivity and care in a sometimes turbulent world.

The Ripple Effect of Positive Energy

When you radiate positive energy, it does not stop with you or the person you directly influence. It reverberates outward, touching friends, families, colleagues, and even strangers. Imagine it as a stone tossed into a tranquil pond. The stone disappears beneath the surface, but circles ripple out, each widening ring impacting a greater area. Positive energy works similarly. A supportive comment you make to someone at

Energy Givers: The Source of Light

breakfast can influence how they treat a co-worker at midday, and that co-worker's uplifted mood may then affect their children in the evening.

In this cascade, you see how your small act can lead to broader transformation. For instance, if you compliment someone's initiative at work, they might feel invigorated and more open to helping a teammate struggling with a project. That teammate might go home feeling accomplished, in turn showing more patience and warmth to family. The family's improved day might encourage them to share kindness with neighbours or friends. This expanding loop of goodwill demonstrates why your seemingly minor actions matter.

Scientifically, emotional contagion helps explain how moods transfer between individuals. Studies suggest that your expression or tone of voice can trigger similar neural responses in those nearby, influencing their emotional states. When you adopt a hopeful, encouraging approach, you can foster a more pleasant social climate wherever you go. Sometimes you may not see the full outcome, but the energy you send out can change a negative situation into a workable one.

You do not need grand gestures to begin a ripple effect. Holding the door for someone or offering a heartfelt "How are you today?" can spark a shift. Suppose the person you engage with has had a rough morning. Your brief kindness might re-centre them enough to avoid an argument with a loved one later. These intangible, subtle effects might be overlooked, but they are real, shaping community morale over time.

Moreover, the ripple effect underscores your sense of responsibility. If you actively spread encouragement, you encourage a chain of positivity. However, if you allow negativity to linger, through harsh words or perpetual complaining, you may trigger a cycle of gloom. Understanding your ability to influence the emotional environment fosters more conscientious behaviour. You choose your words more carefully, realising you hold power that extends beyond the immediate moment.

This concept resonates well in larger group efforts. Imagine you are part of a team trying to accomplish a daunting goal. One person's upbeat attitude can remind everyone that success is possible, spurring renewed effort and resilience. As each member picks up the vibe, the entire team's performance can skyrocket, generating tangible results. Alternatively, a single voice of defeatism can dampen morale, making the path to achievement feel more difficult.

Hence, the ripple effect is an argument for taking ownership of your energy. Yes, circumstances can be bleak, and optimism is not an avoidance of reality but a choice to approach life with constructive perspective. When you do so, your positivity encourages others to shift from hopelessness to problem-solving. It is an unspoken invitation: "Join me in seeing what is possible." Over time, you will notice a changed social atmosphere around you. People may seek you out for your calm demeanour or your supportive presence. This is the ripple effect in action, an ever-expanding wave of positivity that can lighten hearts far beyond your immediate circle.

Balancing Giving and Receiving

Achieving a healthy relationship with an Energy Giver means maintaining a balance between what you offer and what you receive. While it is tempting to rely heavily on their positivity, doing so can create dependency. You risk draining them, leaving the relationship lopsided. Balance is cultivated through mutual respect, thoughtful communication, and consistent reciprocation.

To begin, consider what you bring to the table. You might not have the same endless optimism they do, but you can be a good listener or a reliable confidant. If your friend who is an Energy Giver is going through a tough period, be present. Let them share their uncertainties without rushing them toward a solution. Because they often carry the weight for others, they sometimes yearn for someone to shoulder their burdens. Offer them that safe space.

In practical terms, balancing giving and receiving involves mindful communication. Rather than dumping every worry on them whenever you meet, gauge their mood. Ask how they are doing first. If you sense they have a lot on their plate, it might not be the best time to delve into your own struggles. Wait or find a calmer period. This simple courtesy respects their emotional capacity. Similarly, if they always check on you first, gently prompt them to open up about their day. They might not do so spontaneously, so a direct question can be an excellent starting point.

Another element is self-sufficiency. Aim to develop resilience so you are not entirely reliant on them for emotional soothing. Practice coping skills, like journaling or meditation, to handle minor anxieties or frustrations independently. When you can manage smaller issues alone, you can reserve conversations with them for the more pressing matters that genuinely need another person's perspective. This approach not only prevents overload but also demonstrates that you value their support enough to save it for times you most need it.

Additionally, incorporate gratitude, as covered in earlier sections, to keep reciprocity alive. When they offer assistance or emotional support, thank them sincerely. If possible, return the favour in a way they appreciate. If they have children, maybe you offer a night of babysitting. If they enjoy reading, share a new book you found inspiring. These acts do not have to equal the emotional weight of what they give you, but they reflect thoughtfulness and appreciation.

Sometimes, you might sense tension arising. It may be that the Energy Giver is feeling drained, or that you are uncertain about how to reciprocate. Address these concerns directly. Ask them, "Am I leaning on you too much?" or "How can I support you better?" This openness invites honest feedback, ensuring neither party becomes resentful. A willingness to listen and adapt fosters a genuine balance, strengthening the bond.

Ultimately, balancing giving and receiving nurtures a healthier, longer-lasting connection. It preserves the sense of partnership rather than creating a caretaker dynamic. You remain on equal footing, each person valued for their unique contributions. Though their role as an Energy Giver might be more apparent, your consistent effort to reciprocate and respect boundaries ensures the relationship continues to thrive. You create the sort of supportive synergy that magnifies both your best qualities, shining brighter together than either of you might alone.

Learning from Energy Givers

Energy Givers: The Source of Light

Being around an Energy Giver does more than brighten your day; it can also act as a masterclass in positivity and resilience. You observe how they respond to adversity, remain calm under stress, and maintain a constructive focus in problem-solving. While it might seem like an innate trait, there is usually a disciplined mindset at work. By paying close attention, you can adopt these behaviours, refining them to suit your personality.

Start by noticing how they handle conversations about difficulties. When faced with a challenge, do they panic, or do they calmly assess the situation? Often, they break issues down into manageable steps rather than conflating everything into an insurmountable obstacle. You might learn to do the same: dividing tasks into smaller parts or listing possible solutions, even if the scenario is daunting. Over time, such skills empower you to keep perspective when times get tough.

Another insight you might glean is how they practise self-care. Many Energy Givers recognise the need to recharge, whether through quiet time, hobbies, or other personal pursuits. Some might share how they keep journaling or engage in exercise to release stress. Observing these habits can prompt you to establish your own routines for replenishing energy. If an uplifting friend meditates daily and speaks of its calming influence, you might try it for a month to see if it fosters similar tranquillity.

How they communicate positivity is also instructive. You might notice their focus on what is possible rather than what is lacking. This does not mean ignoring real challenges. Instead, they highlight potential solutions or a lesson learned from a setback. If you want to practise this approach, begin by reframing negative situations. For instance, if your friend complains about a job, guide the conversation toward actionable solutions, or reflect on how this frustration might push them toward better opportunities. Over time, you incorporate the same approach in your dealings.

Energy Givers are often active listeners. Rather than interrupting with their own stories, they let people finish their thoughts. They ask clarifying questions and offer empathy. Study how they use encouraging nods or reflect back the speaker's words to confirm understanding. Practising these techniques can transform you into a more empathetic listener, enhancing your relationships across the board. This shift in how you listen can build deeper bonds, as others sense that you value what they have to say.

Pay attention to how they respond to setbacks. Do they dwell on blame, or do they pivot quickly toward acceptance and moving on? This shift from "Why did this happen to me?" to "What can I do about it now?" is a hallmark of resilient thinkers. If you find yourself ruminating on problems, try consciously shifting your perspective. You might catch yourself mid-complaint and decide to ask, "What is my next best step?" Such a question can break the cycle of negativity.

Lastly, do not forget to communicate your appreciation for their example. Let them know you find their attitude inspiring. Expressing this not only strengthens your bond but also encourages them to continue being that positive force. Over time, you might become an Energy Giver yourself, adopting these learned skills until they blend seamlessly into your own approach. By consciously studying how they navigate life's trials, you collect tools that empower you to remain steady in storms. Ultimately, what you learn from them can ripple forward, enabling you to share that same encouragement with others, creating a multiplied effect of positivity.

The Long-term Benefits of Surrounding Yourself with Positive People

A life lived in the company of uplifting individuals pays dividends for your mental health, relationships, and overall success. Over time, positivity from your circle can shape the lens through which you view the world, nudging you toward optimism, resilience, and greater emotional well-being. Beyond the immediate feel-good effect, you will notice long-term transformations that manifest in multiple areas of your life.

First, consider mental health. Research shows that spending time with positive individuals reduces stress levels, potentially lowering the risk of anxiety and depression. Encouraging friends often helps you process difficulties more calmly, offering a sense of security. Even if challenges persist, you find comfort knowing people believe in your capacity to overcome them. It is like having a steady anchor in turbulent seas, making you less prone to panic. This stable mental environment supports healthy decision-making, stronger motivation, and a sense of peace, no matter your external circumstances.

Next, your broader social network tends to expand more fruitfully. When you engage with Energy Givers, you discover new opportunities for growth, maybe they invite you to events or introduce you to other uplifting folks. Over time, your reputation also improves. You become seen as someone who contributes and encourages. With a positive community behind you, forming new relationships or pursuing new ventures becomes more attainable. Employers or clients may also be drawn to your upbeat demeanour, appreciating your capacity for teamwork and resilience. In turn, you discover new paths for career or personal advancement.

Long-standing positivity in your environment can also improve physical health. While not a direct cure for ailments, emotional well-being can bolster your immune response and encourage healthier lifestyle choices. Surrounded by friends who focus on beneficial habits, such as balanced eating or regular exercise, you may find it easier to adopt similar routines. Over time, your stress-related symptoms may diminish. You might sleep better, experience fewer mood swings, and handle physical discomfort with a better mindset.

Additionally, your confidence flourishes. Affirmation and praise from uplifting friends remind you that your efforts and qualities hold genuine worth. This constant support can embolden you to take calculated risks, such as applying for challenging jobs, learning new skills, or initiating personal projects. You develop faith in your ability to navigate uncharted territory. Growth does not feel scary when you are backed by individuals who believe in you wholeheartedly.

In tandem, these factors pave the way for a brighter future. You respond to challenges with a solution-driven attitude, your personal and professional networks expand, you maintain a healthier mind and body, and you operate with increased self-assurance. One day, you might reflect on your past and see how vital your circle of positivity was in shaping your path. Their influence, subtle day by day, has accumulated into tangible changes in your career, mental state, and even spiritual outlook.

Ultimately, surrounding yourself with positive people is an investment that rewards you in ways both apparent and subtle. In them, you find co-creators of your life's journey, each encouraging you to evolve into a stronger, happier person. As you stand on this foundation of collective optimism, you appreciate that the best version of you was partially nurtured by the uplifting energy of those you chose to keep close. Embracing these relationships for the long haul ensures that your well-being and ambitions remain supported, forming a legacy of positivity that can endure through changing seasons of life.

In Conclusion

Energy Givers uplift, inspire and offer hope. Identifying these radiant souls and fostering bonds with them invites a current of positivity into your life. Through gratitude, balanced interactions, and shared growth, you form a collaboration of mutual support. These relationships, sustained over time, become cornerstones of resilience. Your circle of optimistic friends not only enriches your day-to-day experience but also influences how you face trials.

As you continue, you will explore the opposite side: individuals who leave you drained, the so-called "Energy Vampires." Understanding their traits and learning protection strategies enables you to preserve the equilibrium you have built here. The knowledge you have gained about gratitude, reciprocity, and self-awareness prepares you to handle negative influences without losing the light you have cultivated.

Chapter 3

Energy Vampires: Recognising and Protecting Yourself

In the last chapter, you discovered the role of Energy Givers, those wonderful souls who uplift and revitalise you. It was an exciting reminder of how essential nurturing positivity can be. Yet life also presents another set of connections: Energy Vampires. Unlike Energy Givers, these individuals drain your emotional resources, often leaving you feeling fatigued or burdened. This chapter sheds light on their characteristics, the psychology behind their behaviour, and, importantly, how you can protect yourself while maintaining respect for both yourself and the other person.

By recognising Energy Vampires early and learning how to set boundaries with them, you ensure that your energy remains preserved for the people and activities that matter most. This chapter looks at strategies ranging from straightforward techniques for shielding your emotions to deeper healing approaches. You will learn that even though you cannot change someone else's nature, you can control how you respond. Let us begin by clarifying who these individuals are and what drives their draining behaviour.

Identifying Traits of Energy Vampires

Energy Vampires wear different faces in your life. They can be family members, friends, colleagues, or casual acquaintances. At first glance, they might appear quite ordinary, and some even seem charming or helpful. But over time, you notice a pattern: Each interaction leaves you

Energy Vampires: Recognising and Protecting Yourself

feeling emotionally depleted. Pinpointing this pattern is the first step toward recognising who might be draining you in ways you did not realise.

One common trait is chronic negativity. Energy Vampires regularly highlight the worst in situations, overshadowing any potential positives. You might mention an upcoming holiday, and they respond by warning of potential weather mishaps or other problems that could ruin everything. They rarely discuss solutions. Instead, they linger on complaints and appear unconcerned about improving anything. When you leave the conversation, you might feel your own optimism sapped.

Another sign is excessive complaining without receptiveness to feedback. Complaining once in a while is normal, but Energy Vampires use it as a default mode. They put all their woes on your shoulders yet resist suggestions or attempts to help. If you try to offer a friendly idea or share a similar experience to connect, they ignore it or respond with more reasons why nothing can be fixed. This cycle repeats, turning into a one-sided emotional drain.

Drama is also a recurring theme. Some Energy Vampires appear to stir up conflict wherever they go. They might gossip, pit friends against each other, or blow small misunderstandings out of proportion. This keeps them at the centre of attention, an environment in which they thrive. You might sense tension swirling when they enter the room and feel relief once they leave. Often, you only recognise the weight of their presence in hindsight.

Lack of empathy can be another hallmark. Instead of showing understanding, they might belittle your emotions or dismiss your struggles. For instance, you might confide that you are feeling overwhelmed at work, and they respond by highlighting how their troubles are so much bigger, leaving no room for your viewpoint. This repeated minimisation of your experiences can erode your self-esteem or sense of importance, making you feel overlooked and frustrated.

Some Energy Vampires depend on constant validation. They might call at odd hours, expecting you to listen endlessly. Often, their behaviour can feel manipulative, appearing as subtle guilt trips: "You are the only one who really understands," or "Nobody cares about me but you." These lines can trap you into regular crisis management for them. Recognising this trait is vital because it reveals when someone's demands become unhealthily insistent.

Finally, keep in mind that Energy Vampires are not intrinsically bad individuals. Some are unaware of how their chronic negativity or constant need for validation affects others. Others may carry deep-seated wounds or insecurities, using destructive patterns as a coping mechanism. Recognising their traits allows you to develop empathy for them without sacrificing your energy. Once you identify these consistent patterns, you are better equipped to handle interactions constructively, setting the stage for healthier boundaries and potentially more balanced dynamics.

The Psychological Profile of an Energy Vampire

Many Energy Vampires do not wake up planning to sap others' energy. Their behaviour often stems from deeper psychological layers. Understanding these layers can help you interact with them more effectively while preserving your own well-being. Though there is no single cause that encapsulates every Energy Vampire, certain patterns emerge which illuminate the roots of their draining tendencies.

Often, Energy Vampires struggle with low self-esteem or unresolved emotional pain. This can manifest as a persistent need for reassurance. Unable to soothe their own anxieties, they look outward, leaning on anyone who will listen. Initially, they might appear harmless or simply needy. But as the demands accumulate, you start feeling drained. It can feel as though they have a bottomless well of unhappiness, and your best intentions never fill it. They might not realise their behaviour is smothering you because their focus rests on quelling their internal distress.

Some are accustomed to receiving attention only when in crisis. If past experiences taught them that sympathy or pity is the quickest way to gain validation, they may have normalised drama as their default means of communication. Subconsciously, they conclude that being perpetually overwhelmed or tragic is the only path to being heard. Each meltdown, real or exaggerated, invites the support or pity they crave. You end up acting as their emotional caretaker, and their dependency becomes an unbroken cycle.

Others may exhibit narcissistic tendencies. While narcissism is a complex trait, one aspect is an inflated sense of self-importance coupled with poor empathy. If an individual constantly demands praise, ensures every conversation revolves around them, and dismisses your experiences, you might be dealing with a narcissistic dynamic. They drain you because there is no genuine mutual exchange. Everything is about keeping the spotlight on them, and you are left to comply or risk conflict.

In different cases, unresolved trauma might be at play. Some who have undergone traumatic events develop survival strategies that inadvertently manipulate others. For instance, they might cling to people out of fear of abandonment or create tension and arguments as a maladaptive way of coping with unresolved pain. This does not excuse hurtful behaviour, but understanding it helps clarify the root. By recognising such patterns, you can practise caution, empathy, and boundary-setting rather than letting guilt or frustration override your responses.

A lack of self-awareness is another frequent factor. Many Energy Vampires are not scheming to drain your energy; they simply do not notice how their persistent negativity or demands affect others. They may cycle through friendships, each time losing connections when people feel overloaded. If you attempt to address the issue directly and they seem clueless or defensive, it might be that they have never seriously reflected on their own impact on others.

When you realise that Energy Vampires often operate from psychological vulnerabilities or learned behaviours, it becomes easier to avoid demonising them. However, do not let empathy lead you to self-sacrifice. You can hold understanding for their struggles while taking necessary steps to ensure you do not become collateral damage in their emotional storms. This balance allows you to maintain compassion for their underlying pain without being pulled under by the undertow of their issues. Holding that perspective sets the stage for healthier boundary implementation and ongoing self-care.

Setting Boundaries with Energy Vampires

Energy Vampires: Recognising and Protecting Yourself

Drawing limits with Energy Vampires is an act of respect for both you and them. When you establish clear boundaries, you define how much emotional space you can give without undermining your well-being. This does not mean cutting them off harshly. Instead, think of boundaries as guidelines that preserve your sense of self while still offering a balanced measure of compassion.

Setting boundaries often starts with deciding which topics or situations feel draining. Perhaps you are comfortable discussing career frustrations, but drawn-out conversations about their personal dramas wear you down. If so, plan how you will respond when those draining topics resurface. You can politely shift the conversation. For instance, "I hear what you are going through, but I am not in the right mindset to discuss this right now. Could we maybe talk about something lighter?" This approach is not rude; it is straightforward and honest.

Time boundaries are also important. Maybe you have a friend who calls late at night, reciting a list of problems. If you need rest, or if the conversation consumes hours you do not have, calmly explain that you only answer calls up to a certain time. If they protest, remain polite but firm. Avoid lengthy justifications. For example, "I appreciate you wanting to talk, but I have to be up early. Let us catch up tomorrow at a better time." Though initially awkward, consistent follow-through teaches them that your limit is not flexible.

It is equally important to control face-to-face interactions. If your colleague corners you with gloom each morning, consider gently stating that you need a quiet start to your day. You might say, "I have to prepare myself mentally before diving into conversation. Let us plan a time later?" If they persist, you can simply remind them, "I cannot speak about this now." These boundary statements work best when delivered calmly, without emotional involvement.

Emotional boundaries matter even more. An Energy Vampire may attempt to drag you into their drama. If they start attacking you personally, twisting guilt or blame your way, disengage. End the conversation with a neutral statement like, "I respect your feelings, but I will not be spoken to in that manner. Perhaps we can continue later when we are calmer." No matter their reaction, stay consistent with your boundary. Repeating these steps teaches them that you will not be manipulated by emotional outbursts or guilt trips.

While these measures might feel uncomfortable, remember that healthy relationships require mutual respect. Energy Vampires can sometimes adjust if they genuinely value your connection. Setting firm boundaries can give them a chance to reflect, possibly even grow, if they acknowledge their patterns. If they refuse, then your boundary ensures that you minimise potential harm to yourself. In the long run, your emotional health is a priority. Without your well-being intact, you cannot show up effectively for anyone.

Thus, boundaries are not walls intended to shut people out forever; they are manageable fences that outline how best you can interact without causing yourself lasting harm. Maintaining them consistently sends a clear message that you value your own mental and emotional state. In the best scenarios, you preserve some level of relationship, albeit on terms that keep you balanced and safe from needless exhaustion.

Techniques for Shielding Your Energy

Energy Vampires: Recognising and Protecting Yourself

Even when you have set boundaries with Energy Vampires, situations may arise where you are obliged to interact, such as family functions or workplace collaborations. At these times, shielding your energy becomes essential. By adopting practical techniques to guard your well-being, you ensure that someone else's negativity does not seep into your daily life.

One fundamental approach is visualisation. Take a moment before meeting an Energy Vampire or stepping into a tense space. Close your eyes, breathing in slowly. Picture a soothing light enveloping you like a protective bubble. This simple mental exercise is not a mystical trick. It prompts you to remain centred, to recall that you have control over what you permit into your emotional realm. Keep this image in mind if the conversation starts to drain you. It can help you mentally detach from the negativity.

Next, practise mindfulness of your body. Notice small cues like muscle tension or shallow breathing that signal rising stress. If you catch yourself tensing up, consciously release your shoulders, straighten your posture, and breathe deeply. These shifts might sound small, but they recalibrate your state, preventing you from unconsciously mirroring the other person's tone or agitation.

Selective listening can be invaluable. Energy Vampires often embark on lengthy rants, and responding to each complaint can draw you into their vortex. Instead, you can let them speak while only addressing the points that truly require a response. Politely acknowledging, "I am sorry you are having a tough time," without diving deeply into their negativity, can suffice. You are not ignoring them rudely; you are simply choosing not to immerse yourself in every detail of their complaints.

Another practical tool is time limitation. If you must engage, set a start and end time. Let them know you only have ten minutes before your next appointment or that you can chat until half-past the hour. This timeframe, even if artificial, gives you an escape route to wrap up. Within that timeframe, remain present, but once it is done, politely but definitively bring the conversation to a close. For example, "I appreciate you sharing this, but I have to go now. Let us pause here and catch up later if needed."

Consider neutral topics or a gentle pivot when you sense the conversation growing toxic. A swift change of subject to something less emotionally charged can derail the negativity cycle. You might say, "I understand how stressful this must be. By the way, have you read any good books lately?" or "I heard there is an event happening next week you might find interesting." It might sound abrupt, but it is a skilful tactic to refocus away from draining lines of discussion.

Finally, plan self-care afterwards. If you know a meeting will be stressful, schedule something pleasant immediately after, whether it is a walk, some breathing exercises, or a chat with a friend who has calming energy. This helps you shed residual negativity. By consciously "debriefing" yourself, you avoid carrying tension forward, and you reaffirm that your emotional well-being is your responsibility. Over time, these habits equip you with robust defences, letting you interact with Energy Vampires on your own terms without depleting your vital energy reserves.

The Importance of Emotional Detox

Energy Vampires: Recognising and Protecting Yourself

Interacting with Energy Vampires can leave an emotional residue behind, even after you have parted ways. It might feel like a heaviness or unsettled angst that lingers, influencing your thoughts and mood. Enter the concept of emotional detox, a conscious method of releasing negative energies that accumulate in you. While we often think of detox in terms of diet, emotional detox serves to cleanse mental clutter, allowing you to reset and reclaim balance.

This process starts with awareness. Immediately after a draining interaction, take a mental note of how you feel. Are you irritable, tense, or simply subdued? Acknowledging these feelings is not about wallowing in negativity. Rather, it is about affirming that your emotions have shifted from your usual baseline. Gently thinking, "Yes, I feel anxious right now," can stop you from suppressing it or ignoring it. Recognition is the first step toward letting go.

Expressing yourself is another key. If you bottle up annoyance or worry, it may solidify, morphing into long-term stress or even resentment. Instead, consider venting in a healthy way, through journaling, talking with a trusted confidant, or using creative outlets like sketching or music. By naming and articulating your emotions, you keep them from festering. You could write a letter you never send, describing exactly how that draining individual made you feel. This process helps you release tension and clarifies your thoughts.

A helpful extension of emotional detox involves grounding activities. Grounding might mean walking in a local park, where you tune into the sensation of grass underfoot or the breeze against your skin. It could be as simple as practising slow, measured breathing. Breathe in for a few counts, hold briefly, and then exhale for the same number of counts. This stabilises your body's stress responses, reminding you that you are not defined by someone else's negativity.

Visual or guided imagery can also deepen the effect. Some people imagine washing away negativity in the shower, envisioning the water cleansing the residue of negative interactions. Others find that lighting a candle or listening to tranquil music helps them shift their internal atmosphere. It may feel odd at first, but such rituals help anchor your intention to discard the emotional burden you carry from that draining conversation.

Another aspect is replenishing with positivity. Rather than trying solely to flush out negativity, replace it with something uplifting. Chat with someone who makes you laugh, watch a short comedy clip, or listen to motivational podcasts. The infusion of positivity reminds you that negativity is not the only force at play. You have the power to cultivate lighter emotions. Over time, repeatedly choosing positive interactions helps you internalise the perspective that you can rebalance after negativity.

Finally, emotional detox is more than a quick fix; it is an ongoing practice. You may not achieve a perfect sense of calm after one session. Keep applying these methods whenever needed. The goal is to minimise how long you remain weighed down. If you consistently care for your emotional health in this way, you will become ever more adept at recovering from draining episodes. The next time an Energy Vampire attempts to steal your peace, you will be ready, confident in your ability to reconnect with your inner equilibrium.

Energy Vampires: Recognising and Protecting Yourself

Managing Relationships with Energy Vampires in the Workplace and Family

Workplaces and families can pose special challenges. In a job setting, you cannot simply avoid a draining colleague if you share assignments or daily interactions. Similarly, if the Energy Vampire in question is a parent, sibling, or in-law, fully distancing yourself may not feel feasible, especially if you are committed to upholding family ties. Yet even in these spheres, you can protect your well-being while treating others with respect.

At work, clarity is paramount. When a colleague regularly oversteps, such as dumping tasks on you or using every break for negativity, set boundaries early. You might say, "I appreciate your updates, but I need to finish my own tasks first. Let us revisit this after lunch." Maintaining a professional tone guards you from being perceived as cold or dismissive, yet it firmly signals your limits. If the negativity persists, document instances to ensure you have evidence if you ever need to discuss matters with a supervisor. Many workplaces have policies designed to address harassment or ongoing tension, so do not hesitate to seek assistance from human resources if necessary.

Family dynamics can be more complicated due to emotional history. If you have an overly critical sibling, you might feel compelled to respond politely, even though each barbed comment bites. One approach is a technique known as the "broken record." Calmly and consistently repeat your boundary. If they belittle your choices, calmly affirm, "I respect your view, but I have made my decision," or "I do not wish to discuss this further." Over time, they may reduce such remarks, seeing you will not be drawn into an argument.

Plan ahead for gatherings. If you know a family member often brings drama to holiday dinners, consider putting some protective strategies in place. For example, coordinate with a supportive relative to steer you away from tense conversations or volunteer to help in the kitchen when you sense negativity brewing. Such small steps can defuse tension before it escalates, reducing emotional strain. If distance or short, controlled visits become necessary, do not feel guilty. Setting limitations is sometimes the healthiest choice to preserve the relationship in the long run.

Honesty can help with certain relatives or colleagues who might be unaware of how their behaviour hurts you. Gently explaining, "I feel drained when our talks revolve around criticisms or gossip," might open their eyes. Some might be defensive initially, but if they value your connection, they might try to change. Approach this honestly yet kindly, avoiding accusatory tones like, "You are always so negative." Instead, frame it around your feelings: "I notice I become anxious after these interactions, and I would like us to communicate differently."

Professional counselling or mediation can be an option, especially in a family context where repeated conflicts occur. Sometimes, an outside perspective helps everyone see that certain patterns are unsustainable. If the other person rejects this, you can still attend counselling on your own to clarify your next steps and build resilience. Taking these actions underscores your commitment to mental well-being, ensuring you do not lose yourself in an unending cycle of negativity.

Energy Vampires: Recognising and Protecting Yourself

Ultimately, even in intricate environments like the workplace or extended family, you can find workable approaches to minimise energy drain. Be firm but fair, remain consistent in asserting your limits, and, above all, remember you hold the choice of how to respond. Though you cannot tailor someone else's behaviour, you can shape how you engage with it, preserving a sense of calm and self-respect in the face of ongoing negativity.

Healing from the Effects of Energy Vampires

Encountering Energy Vampires can inflict lasting emotional effects, especially if you have endured repeated draining episodes. You might feel resentful, doubting your worth, or second-guessing whether you have the right to assert boundaries. Over time, these experiences can chip away at your self-esteem. Healing is about reclaiming your sense of self, reminding yourself that you deserve relationships rooted in respect and genuine care.

One powerful strategy is to focus on self-validation. Remind yourself that setting boundaries does not equate to selfishness. It is part of self-preservation. Create simple affirmations to read in the morning or before bed. For example, "I am worthy of balanced, respectful relationships," or "I am permitted to protect my emotional health." These statements guide you toward a mindset where you believe wholeheartedly that you deserve better.

Therapy or counselling can be transformative in your healing journey. A professional can offer objective insights, helping you dissect why certain interactions trigger you so intensely. They also supply coping strategies you might not have considered. Sometimes, just speaking to someone impartial can alleviate the mental load, enabling you to find clarity. Whether your experiences stem from family patterns, romantic connections, or workplace conflicts, a counsellor can provide valuable tools to foster resilience.

Being part of a supportive group is also instrumental. Seek out a circle of encouraging friends or mentors. If you have recently broken free from a draining relationship, these peers can remind you how healthy reciprocity looks and feels. Sharing experiences with others who understand can speed up the healing process by validating your emotions. Whether it is an informal support circle or an established local group, connecting with people on similar journeys can be comforting. Simply knowing you are not alone offers strength.

Another dimension to consider is forgiving yourself for allowing repeated negativity. You might look back and think, "Why did I tolerate that for so long?" or "I should have spoken up sooner." This self-blame can become an internal weight. Yet, it is unproductive. At the time, you did the best you could with the emotional tools you had. Forgiving yourself allows you to move forward without lingering regret. From that vantage point, you can adopt new strategies more confidently.

Mind-body interventions can further assist your healing. Activities that integrate emotional release with physical awareness, like yoga, dance, or even hiking, unlock tensions stored in the body. Writing in a journal about your experiences can help you reflect on the growth you have achieved. Tracking small improvements, such as going a week without letting someone's negativity dominate your thoughts, encourages you to see progress. As you accumulate such milestones, your sense of emotional security strengthens.

Finally, keep in mind that healing does not mean erasing painful memories; it involves redefining them. Perhaps your experiences taught you the necessity of boundaries. You learned how resilient you can be. Reframe your story from that perspective: "I faced draining relationships and emerged wiser." Through this lens, the process of healing becomes a reclaiming of power. You step beyond victimhood and into a newfound sense of autonomy, carrying lessons that enhance your future connections rather than hinder them.

Transformative Conversations: Dealing with Energy Vampires

Though some Energy Vampires remain unchanged, there are moments when an honest conversation can spark transformation. This depends on the individual's willingness to reflect on their actions. If you suspect the person might be receptive, a direct yet empathetic exchange can sometimes encourage them to adopt healthier ways of relating. Here, communication becomes a powerful vehicle for mutual growth.

Preparing is half the battle. If you choose to address the issue, be clear about your intentions: you aim to improve the relationship, not to condemn them. Rehearse how you might introduce the topic in a calm tone. For instance, "I value our friendship, and I have noticed an ongoing pattern that leaves me feeling exhausted," or "I care about you but feel we fall into negativity more than either of us wants." By starting with positive regard, you set the conversation on a cooperative note, reducing the likelihood of defensiveness.

Using personal statements helps avoid blame. Instead of declaring, "You always bring drama," try, "I find it difficult when our conversations frequently revolve around conflicts. It leaves me feeling tense." This approach emphasises your feelings and experiences rather than accusing them. They are more apt to listen if they do not sense an immediate attack. Keep your statements concise and direct, offering real-life examples: "On Tuesday, when we talked for two hours about how everyone treats you unfairly, I felt anxious afterwards."

Next, propose potential solutions or guidelines. Explain the changes you hope to see in your dynamic. Perhaps you want a more balanced conversation ratio: sometimes discussing their life, sometimes discussing yours, and sometimes discussing mutual interests. If negativity is the problem, suggest a small shift, such as also discussing possible solutions or highlights of the day. For instance, "I would love to hear about anything positive happening in your life as well, so we do not focus on difficulties alone."

Be ready for resistance. Energy Vampires might react with denial, self-pity, or even anger. Calmly reiterate your points if they appear defensive. Emphasise your willingness to maintain the bond in a healthier manner. If they become combative, end the discussion for the time being, reminding them you are open to talking again later. Displaying your boundaries consistently is key. Without follow-through, your conversation will lack impact.

Offer reassurance that you are not expecting perfection overnight. Changes in deep-set behaviour take time. But do hold them accountable. If they slip into the same patterns next time, gently bring it up: "Remember our chat about balancing our conversations? Can we try switching gears now?" This consistent prompting can help them build self-awareness.

Finally, stay prepared for any outcome. Some individuals might embrace the opportunity to shift. They could thank you for your honesty or begin to consciously moderate their negativity. In time, you might see notable improvements, forging a more authentic, uplifting relationship. Others might balk, refusing to see any fault in their behaviour. If that happens, remind yourself that you tried. At that stage, the best path might involve stricter boundaries to avoid further emotional drain. Nonetheless, you have given them a fair chance to grow, making your next decisions grounded in respect for both of you.

The Role of Forgiveness in Releasing Negative Connections

When an Energy Vampire has caused consistent distress, you might feel anger or resentment welling up inside. While boundaries are crucial in limiting future harm, you might also need to release emotional baggage through forgiveness. This step is frequently misunderstood. Forgiveness does not mean excusing inappropriate behaviour or allowing someone back into your life without conditions. Rather, it involves letting go of the emotional burden that resentment creates so you can move forward in peace.

The first step is acknowledging that grudges keep you tied to the very negativity you are trying to escape. If you catch yourself replaying scenarios where they belittled or drained you, that is your mind clinging to past harm. This can perpetuate the emotional toll, even if you have physically distanced yourself. Forgiveness, in this sense, becomes an act of self-liberation. You choose to stop granting them free space in your head.

A practical approach is to separate the person from their actions. People adopt draining behaviours for a variety of reasons. Some are shaped by trauma, mental struggles, or a lack of healthy coping strategies. Observing these factors does not justify their actions, but it can shift your perspective from personalising the harm to understanding that they are stuck in negative cycles. When you see them this way, forgiveness arises more naturally, as you empathise with their struggles while still refusing to excuse the hurt they caused.

Journaling can be helpful. Take time to articulate the emotions or memories that remain painful. Write them down clearly, capturing all the anger and betrayal you may still harbour. Once you have laid it out, compose another page where you explore your desire to let go. Statements such as, "I choose to release the hurt so I can find peace," can cement your resolve. This process often brings clarity, underscoring that you can hold compassion for them while safeguarding yourself.

Sometimes, direct communication might facilitate forgiveness, although it depends on the situation. If you sense the person is open to hearing how they wronged you, you might share your feelings, emphasising that you do not necessarily want to reopen the relationship but to find closure. They may apologise or offer explanations, which might or might not help. Either way, your main aim is to voice your perspective and release lingering anger.

It is also valuable to remember self-forgiveness. Maybe you are mad at yourself for "allowing" prolonged drain or for not speaking up sooner. Recognise that you navigated those interactions with the knowledge, courage, or readiness you had at the time. Dwelling on what you "should have" done can hold you hostage to guilt. Freeing yourself from that guilt is as essential as forgiving the other person.

Ultimately, forgiveness fosters emotional freedom, paving the way for a more hopeful mindset. Whether you maintain a distant civil relationship with the Energy Vampire or opt for no contact at all, releasing bitterness is an act of self-care. By dissolving negative emotional ties, you reclaim the energy you once lost to anger. You step forward lighter, leaving behind the heavy baggage of unresolved conflict and preserving mental space for healthier, more positive connections.

Empowerment: Taking Back Your Energy

Empowerment is the final step once you have identified, managed, and healed from Energy Vampire interactions. It signifies reclaiming your own strength, acknowledging that you have the right to direct your emotional resources. Rather than feeling like a victim, constantly at the mercy of others' negativity, you decide how much energy you give away and to whom. This shift in perspective lifts you from passive acceptance to active control, reshaping how you navigate all relationships.

One powerful way to practice empowerment is through self-affirmation. Each morning, spend a few minutes stating truths about yourself: "I choose to protect my energy today," or "I am strong enough to handle negativity without letting it define me." Repeating these statements might feel awkward initially, but it gradually cements the idea that you have autonomy over your emotional well-being. Rather than letting daily events toss you around, you command how your emotions are channelled.

Another aspect of empowerment is harnessing your personal interests and creativity. If you have neglected your hobbies due to emotional exhaustion, now is the time to reignite them. Whether painting, cooking, or exploring a new sport, these activities remind you that life is multi-dimensional. Rather than revolving around a draining person's drama, your life can revolve around passion and growth. This self-directed focus prevents your sense of identity from getting entangled in someone else's chaos.

Remember that empowerment does not rule out compassion. You can remain empathetic to an Energy Vampire's struggles while preserving your boundaries. If you choose to engage, you do so from a place of strength rather than obligation or fear. This perspective means you no longer see them as an undefeatable force. They are simply an individual with flaws, and you have developed strategies to keep your personal peace intact.

Surrounding yourself with supportive individuals magnifies your empowerment. Spend more time with the friends or family members who reciprocate your positivity. Engaging in conversations that uplift you affirms that negativity does not define your social world. Creating these pockets of emotional nourishment fortifies you so that when you do encounter an Energy Vampire, you have the resilience to remain composed and unaffected.

Measuring growth is also motivating. Reflect on how you once handled draining episodes, perhaps with silent frustration or guilt-laden compliance. Compare that to how

Energy Vampires: Recognising and Protecting Yourself

you respond now, with clear boundaries and calm self-assurance. Observe how much less time you spend ruminating on negativity. Maybe you no longer dread phone calls from certain individuals, or you bounce back more quickly after a tense family gathering. These small victories confirm that you have shifted from being drained to being in control.

Taking back your energy is not a one-time event but a continuing process. There will be days you feel fully in charge and days you slip into old habits. Rather than seeing occasional setbacks as failures, frame them as reminders to keep using your skills. Over time, your empowered stance becomes second nature, weaving into every area of your life. You discover that even if negativity surfaces, it cannot overshadow your power to cultivate inner calm and maintain fulfilling relationships. And that sense of self-guided strength sets the stage for a future where your energy remains firmly yours, to be shared at your discretion, not siphoned without your consent.

In Conclusion

You have explored the realm of Energy Vampires and how to respond effectively. From understanding their traits to setting boundaries and engaging in emotional detox, you are now equipped to remain centred no matter who you encounter. Recognising that such negativity often stems from deeper psychological roots can encourage empathy, but never at the expense of your well-being. By protecting and reclaiming your energy, you become more resilient.

The next chapter addresses the idea of finding and cultivating your tribe. Having worked through the drainers in your life, you are well-prepared to seek out and sustain relationships that genuinely nurture you. Remember: preserving your well-being is not selfish. It paves the way for living wholeheartedly and attracting the companionship and support you truly deserve.

Chapter 4

The Quest for Your Tribe

Human beings have always been communal, looking for kinship and acceptance. You might discover that it is not blood ties but shared values and mutual goals that truly make you feel at home. In this chapter, you explore the concept of your tribe, those who understand, support, and encourage you. Previously, you learned about both positive and negative influences on your well-being, so now it is time to actively build a circle of like-minded individuals who enrich your life.

Your tribe does not have to be large. Even a handful of people who "get" you can make all the difference in feeling secure and purposeful. Whether you find your tribe through a mutual passion, a life stage, or a shared worldview, the key is intentional connection. You decide who you welcome into your circle and how you develop those friendships. Let us begin by defining what modern "tribe" means and why it matters in a busy, fragmented world.

Defining "Tribe" in the Modern Age

The word "tribe" calls to mind ancient communities bound by geography and survival needs. In the modern age, the word stands for a chosen family of individuals who resonate with your core values, regardless of blood ties. You see glimpses of this new concept in social groups, community circles, and online forums. The link that unifies them is not forced tradition but deliberate connection, grounded in mutual respect and empathy.

Connections

A modern tribe can arise around shared passions, such as a love of fitness, reading, or creative pursuits. You might meet monthly at a local group or interact daily via an online platform. Over time, these connections surpass interest-based chats, developing into genuine support systems. Perhaps you start as strangers, but repeated interactions foster trust, jokes, and a sense of solidarity. Another key aspect is emotional support. Traditional tribes offered communal protection, from raising children to harvesting crops. Today, your emotional well-being may be similarly bolstered by a small band of people you can call upon when life unravels. Whether it is confiding about a bad day or celebrating a career success, your tribe shares in life's extremes, reinforcing a sense that you are never truly alone.

Social media has influenced how tribes form. You can now connect with people scattered across different continents, united by a single passion or cause. But forming a true tribe requires effort beyond clicking a follow button. Meaningful ties occur when people consistently interact, share personal stories, and show up for each other. You might find yourself having more genuine discussions in a small, focused online group than in vast open forums. Authenticity and trust become the linchpins of these digital tribes.

One challenge of forming a tribe today involves the fast pace of life. Many people juggle packed schedules, leaving minimal time for deeper bonding. But your tribe does not need constant in-person contact to flourish. Monthly meetups or consistent online gatherings can suffice, provided there is real commitment. The point is the quality of interaction rather than the quantity. A single conversation where you truly feel heard might outweigh multiple shallow get-togethers.

The Quest for Your Tribe

You also want to be mindful of inclusivity. If your group becomes too rigid, focused only on your exact viewpoint, you risk forming an echo chamber. True tribal bonds evolve when members bring diverse insights. You benefit from a variety of life experiences, broadening your outlook. At the same time, shared values remain the bedrock that fosters emotional safety. You agree on principles like kindness, honesty, or loyalty, giving your group a strong ethical framework.

Thus, while the old notion of a tribe tied to ancestral roots may have diminished, the craving to belong to a supportive community remains. This new tribe is flexible, formed through choice rather than forced circumstance. Despite the digital era's complexities, such close-knit circles bring meaning. They become anchors in your journey, reminding you that you are part of something bigger than yourself, and that you have companions ready to uplift you. By recognising and embracing your tribe, you affirm the enduring power of human connection in the modern world.

The Significance of Finding Your Tribe

Finding your tribe answers a deep human need for belonging. From infancy, you rely on caregivers, friends, and the broader community for security and affirmation. Yet as you grow older, you learn that not everyone understands you. Some acquaintances serve practical purposes but do not share your deeper convictions or aspirations. Others might undervalue your passions. This can leave you feeling isolated, prompting a search for people who truly see you.

The tribe you choose helps fill that void. When you are with them, you sense alignment, a relief that you do not need to water yourself down or pretend to be someone else. You can be open about the things you love, whether obscure music, hiking, scientific debates, or anything else. In turn, you bond through a shared sense of enthusiasm and respect for differences. This synergy fosters growth and self-confidence. No longer do you feel like the "odd one out"; you have a place where you fit.

Belonging to a tribe also offers resilience. Life events, job losses, health challenges, relationship endings, can test your emotional fortitude. In these times, your tribe acts as a buffer. They rally around you, offering suggestions, comfort, and in some cases tangible assistance. Their presence can make daunting situations feel a bit more bearable. You see you are not struggling alone. That knowledge alone can energise you, providing the courage to keep going.

The significance extends beyond just providing emotional safety. Your tribe can spark creativity and ambition. Sharing goals and experiences can open your eyes to possibilities you never considered. A conversation with a driven friend might inspire you to take a leap at work. Observing a tribe member turn a hobby into a thriving venture might encourage you to do the same. When you feel that sense of camaraderie, it fuels your ambition to pursue dreams confidently.

A key facet of tribal belonging is accountability. People in your tribe want the best for you. If you deviate from your personal standards or appear overwhelmed, they can gently nudge you back on track. It feels supportive, as opposed to judgemental. For instance, if you have declared your goal of writing regularly, your tribe might check in: "How is your writing going?" That question alone can keep you motivated, knowing they genuinely care about your progress.

The Quest for Your Tribe

Moreover, finding a tribe can reduce loneliness. Despite living in a highly connected age, many wrestle with feelings of isolation. Having your tribe means always having a place to turn, a group that welcomes you without preconditions. This reduces the emotional burden of external rejections or failures. It reminds you that your value as a person is not measured by accomplishments alone.

Overall, the significance lies in nurturing a sense of unity while preserving individuality. In a healthy tribe, members encourage each other to bloom in unique ways rather than conform to a single mould. This synergy fosters an environment of mutual respect, inspiration, and unwavering support. Therefore, discovering your tribe is not merely an enhancement to life; it can become the very bedrock of emotional well-being, letting you express who you are with others who wholeheartedly celebrate you.

Steps to Discovering Your Tribe

Finding your tribe often seems like stumbling upon a rare treasure, but there are practical steps to increase your chances of discovery. Start by clarifying who you are and what you value. Honest self-exploration helps you understand the environments or interests around which you might meet like-minded souls. Perhaps you enjoy fitness, artistic pursuits, or volunteering. Identify these interests and reflect on how they align with your ideals. Such self-awareness guides your search toward communities that share your outlook.

Next, step outside your comfort zone. It is easy to dream about meeting new companions but never actually show up anywhere new. While it might be daunting, take the initiative to attend local meetups, community events, or group classes relevant to your hobbies or profession. Online platforms can also be a gateway. Join groups dedicated to your interests. The virtual realm can lead to offline connections, too. The key is consistent participation rather than a one-off appearance.

Active engagement is crucial. When you attend a workshop or a discussion group, avoid standing on the sidelines. Contribute to conversations, ask genuine questions, and be receptive to meeting people. If a group meets regularly, try to attend multiple sessions to build familiarity. Over time, you and others become comfortable around each other, increasing the likelihood of authentic bonds forming.

Once you begin mingling, stay open-minded. You might not instantly click with everyone, but do not dismiss potential connections prematurely. Sometimes, deeper common ground emerges after initial polite chats. Rather than focusing on superficial differences, notice who displays kindness, shared humour, or similar passions. Often, the best relationships evolve naturally as mutual understanding grows. Keep in mind that your aim is not to impress everyone but to find those with whom you can genuinely relate.

Communication skills matter, too. Being approachable and attentive to others' stories makes a great difference. Instead of always steering conversations to your experiences, show curiosity in their backgrounds. Ask follow-up questions when someone mentions a personal project or dream. This approach fosters mutual trust, as people see you value their perspective. That trust can lay the foundation for future meetups or even deeper alliances.

Lastly, allow time for trial and error. Finding a tribe is rarely instantaneous. Some groups may turn out to be less compatible than expected. Others might start promisingly but fade if schedules conflict. Rather than feeling defeated, remain flexible. Each attempt teaches you more about what you seek in a tribe, whether it is a focus on self-development or a shared cultural interest. Patience is key, as strong communities develop organically.

In sum, your journey begins with self-knowledge, followed by proactive steps to engage in relevant communities. Keep an open mind about who you might meet, practise genuine communication, and understand that not every encounter leads to immediate friendship. By persisting kindly and consistently, you raise the odds of discovering that group of companions who resonate with your heart and your goals, forming a true tribe that enriches every aspect of your life.

Building Meaningful Connections within Your Tribe

Once you have located or begun forming your tribe, the real work of building meaningful connections starts. A shared interest or cause may bring you together, but forging deeper emotional bonds requires consistent effort, kindness, and a willingness to invest in others' lives. Think of your tribe as a growing circle where everyone's stories and perspectives matter.

Listening with intent is a cornerstone. Rather than treating conversations as a chance to wait for your turn to speak, engage fully. If someone is discussing a personal struggle, reflect their words back to them. For example, "I sense how stressful that must be," or "It sounds like you have been under a lot of pressure." These responses show you are not just hearing but genuinely absorbing what they share. Over time, that level of empathy prompts them to see you as trustworthy and supportive.

Open communication also involves honesty. If you disagree, express it respectfully. Instead of silent nods, you could say, "I see your point. I have a slightly different perspective, though." This fosters an environment where everyone feels comfortable voicing personal views without fear of judgment or ridicule. True tribes do not shy away from constructive disagreements; they handle them with empathy and an open mind, often emerging stronger on the other side.

Shared experiences deepen bonds. You might organise group projects or outings that tap into your common interests, from nature hikes to cooking sessions. These activities spark memories that become a communal narrative. The laughter and challenges faced together forge emotional ties that are hard to replicate in mere online chats. Physical presence is not strictly necessary if you are in a long-distance circle, though. Virtual collaborations, like working on a shared creative idea or completing an online course together, can still offer that sense of team spirit.

Regular check-ins are essential. Setting up small rituals, for example, a weekly phone call, a monthly coffee meet-up, or a group message thread, keeps you connected. If a tribe member has a big exam or an important job interview, text them good luck beforehand or see how it went afterwards. These small gestures convey that their endeavours matter to you. You build a tapestry (avoiding restricted word) of micro-moments, each reaffirming the care and unity within your circle.

Respect for boundaries is crucial. Every individual within your tribe has personal limits and obligations outside the group. If someone declines an invitation or needs alone time, honour that. Relationships thrive when each person feels their boundaries are seen and respected. You can also avoid over-dependence on a single person by rotating responsibilities, ensuring that no one member carries an undue burden, whether it is always hosting gatherings or consistently providing solutions to group issues.

Lastly, practise mutual uplift. Celebrate a friend's successes wholeheartedly. If one member lands a promotion, share in their excitement with a heartfelt congratulations. If someone faces a setback, encourage them with sincere understanding. This atmosphere of shared celebration and empathy fosters loyalty. Over time, your tribe becomes a source of emotional shelter for everyone involved. Together, you face life's ups and downs, each person buoyed by the knowledge they have a supportive network standing by them. This synergy transforms casual acquaintances into lifelong collaborators on each other's journeys.

The Role of Shared Values and Beliefs in Tribal Connections

Shared values and beliefs often serve as the foundation of strong tribal bonds. While you can find common ground in hobbies or professional pursuits, it is a deeper alignment of principles that cements truly cohesive relationships. Values such as integrity, loyalty, or kindness imbue your group with unity. When you gather around these shared ideals, trust naturally flourishes.

It helps to articulate which values matter to you. If honesty is paramount, for instance, a tribe where people conceal or distort the truth will eventually leave you unsettled. Alternatively, if you esteem resilience and personal growth, you may connect best with individuals who embrace self-improvement and encourage it in one another. By understanding your key principles, you refine your search for a group that resonates with them.

Shared beliefs do not necessarily require uniformity, however. A tribe can be diverse in religious views, cultural backgrounds, or political leanings, as long as core principles, such as compassion or open-mindedness, remain. This nuanced balance of similarities and differences enriches conversations, offering varied perspectives but still anchored by mutual respect. If everyone thinks exactly the same, you risk echo chambers. A healthy tribe challenges you to sharpen your ideas while respecting the group's unifying values.

Conflict is not eliminated by shared values, but it does become more manageable. Suppose your group prizes empathy. When disagreements arise, each party is reminded to handle them compassionately. Even if you hold opposing viewpoints, the underlying rule of kindness prompts you to address differences constructively. This sense of unity in shared ideals can transform potential rifts into opportunities for deeper understanding.

Rituals reinforce these shared beliefs. For instance, if environmental stewardship is important, your tribe might organise monthly clean-up events or adopt sustainable habits together. Such collective actions not only strengthen the sense of unity but also give you tangible reminders that you are aligned in purpose. In time, these group rituals deepen emotional ties because they reflect genuine commitment, not mere words.

Sometimes you may discover mismatch in core values as you get to know each other more intimately. Perhaps you believed you aligned with someone, only to find they prioritise competition over collaboration. Rather than forcing the bond, it might be wise to accept that your deeper principles do not match. Better to maintain a cordial acquaintance than to attempt an inauthentic closeness that leaves you dissatisfied. Being part of a tribe is voluntary, so if a clash arises that cannot be bridged respectfully, you can choose a healthier distance.

In day-to-day life, shared values yield countless benefits. Decisions about how to spend time, how to handle conflict, or which causes to support become more fluid when everyone's core principles overlap. You are not constantly negotiating fundamental differences. Instead, you operate on a mutual understanding: "We are on the same page about what truly matters." That feeling of moral and philosophical harmony fosters genuine affection and reliability. Over time, you see that your collective strength grows from the firm ground of beliefs you all cherish. This unshakeable foundation allows your tribe to face life's storms with unity and unwavering resolve.

Navigating Differences Within Your Tribe

Even the closest tribes face differences, as each member has unique opinions, experiences, and preferences. Disagreements may arise about how to handle finances in a shared endeavour or how to address a sensitive topic. Though these conflicts can feel uncomfortable, they present opportunities to strengthen bonds through open communication and mutual respect.

First, normalise the existence of differences. It is unrealistic to expect perfect harmony at all times. When you acknowledge that variances in perspective are inevitable, conflicts become less surprising and more approachable. People are less likely to overreact, and more inclined to solve disagreements cooperatively. Remind yourself that your tribe's diversity of thought can be a blessing. It brings creativity and balance, provided everyone approaches these differences constructively.

Active listening is vital. Instead of rushing to defend your viewpoint, focus on understanding the other person's stance. Ask clarifying questions: "What is it about this plan that concerns you?" or "Could you explain more about where your idea comes from?" This approach fosters empathy. The person feels heard, which can diffuse tension. In some cases, you might realise their perspective has merit. Even if you ultimately disagree, you have honoured their input, which goes a long way toward preserving goodwill.

Avoid personal attacks or condescending language. Aim to phrase feedback as "I" statements: "I feel this approach might overlook some details," or "I am worried about how the cost affects the group." You voice your concerns without implying the other party is ignorant or misguided. Minimising blame sets a calmer tone for dialogue. If emotions run high, taking a short break to gather thoughts is often helpful.

Seek compromise where possible. If two members disagree on an event location, maybe rotate choices or split tasks. If the issue is more profound, like a moral debate, find smaller areas of agreement. In some situations, tribe members might need to "agree to disagree" while upholding overall respect. The process matters more than the final outcome. By managing disagreements fairly, you reinforce trust that everyone can remain amicable despite diverging opinions.

Respect boundaries if certain topics repeatedly spark disputes. If a friend is unwavering in a political or lifestyle stance, continuously clashing about it can erode warmth in the group. You might collectively decide that some matters remain personal choices, and not the tribe's domain to fix. This does not bury issues; it merely respects that not all matters require unanimous agreement. If the difference is fundamentally irreconcilable and greatly impacts group harmony, you may choose to loosen ties with that member or redefine the nature of your bond.

Above all, emphasise preserving the relationship over winning an argument. If your tribe is anchored in shared values like empathy and honesty, conflicts can serve as a reminder of why you came together in the first place. The trust you have built helps you navigate turmoil, emerging stronger and more cohesive. As you move on from disagreements, reflect on what was learned. Often, tackling differences well fosters deeper connections, enhancing the tribe's collective resilience and sense of unity.

The Impact of Technology on Tribal Connections

Technology reshapes how tribes form and function. Gone are the days when you relied purely on face-to-face interactions to find like-minded companions. Now, social media platforms, online groups, and instant messaging link you to communities around the globe. If used judiciously, these tools let you maintain relationships with people who share your passions and beliefs, even if they live across continents.

Online platforms can act as a powerful catalyst for discovering your tribe. Perhaps you are fascinated by a niche interest, like restoring vintage cars or composing choral music, that few around you appreciate. In moments, you can join a digital group where enthusiastic strangers become friends. These shared interests lay the groundwork for conversation and can lead to deeper emotional connections, particularly as you engage in ongoing dialogues, exchanging tips, stories, and humour.

However, technology can also breed superficial ties if you rely solely on likes and brief texts. Your interactions may remain shallow, never delving into genuine emotional exchange. Real tribe-building calls for more authentic engagement. Consider smaller online gatherings or group video calls for a more personal approach. Encourage the group to share personal experiences and insights, not just curated images or highlights. This fosters emotional authenticity in a medium known for surface-level interactions.

Another upside of technology is convenience. Busy schedules and geographical barriers can hamper you from meeting in person. Online check-ins, whether via group chats or scheduled virtual sessions, keep the communal spirit alive. Imagine that your closest tribe members reside in different time zones. Through a messaging app, you can still share daily updates or achievements, bridging distances with ongoing warmth and encouragement. Despite physical separation, the sense of togetherness remains strong.

Challenges do arise. Misunderstandings are likelier when relying on typed text devoid of tone and nonverbal cues. A simple remark can be misread as sarcastic or dismissive. Over time, unresolved tensions might escalate, particularly if members do not clarify ambiguous messages. Making use of video or voice calls can reduce the risk of misinterpretation. If conflict arises, address it quickly with a phone chat or video meeting to clear up confusion.

In addition, technology's constant presence can lead to burnout or overexposure. Endless notifications might hinder your ability to be fully present with family or in tasks needing concentration. Setting boundaries around device usage can protect your mental health. For instance, you could agree with your online tribe to pause messaging after a certain hour, or to keep group discussions focused and respectful, avoiding incessant pings.

Despite these pitfalls, technology remains a valuable ally for tribe-building. It grants unprecedented access to diverse communities, letting you transcend physical limitations to find those who resonate with you. With mindful usage, you can maintain a healthy balance between digital and offline worlds. By combining authenticity, respect, and consistent engagement, you can create vibrant communal ties that truly mirror a tribe's essence, support, empathy, and shared growth, amplified by technology's connective power rather than overshadowed by its potential drawbacks.

Cultivating a Sense of Belonging

Feeling genuinely included within a tribe transcends merely being present. You can attend every gathering and still sense isolation if deeper connections do not form. Belonging is about emotional security, the sense that you are valued for who you are rather than for superficial traits or what you can do for others. This sense of belonging provides an anchor in a fast-paced, sometimes impersonal world.

One way to foster belonging is through consistent participation. Showing up regularly helps your presence become woven into the group. Whether in-person or online, consistency signals commitment. Others begin to count on you, and in turn, you learn more about them. Through repeated interactions, you share stories, inside jokes, or group traditions that build collective identity. If you often skip out or only drop by briefly, you may miss these bonding moments.

Vulnerability also plays a role. Trust can only deepen if you share a bit of yourself, your aspirations, struggles, or silly habits. By lowering your guard, you signal that you trust others, inviting them to reciprocate. The result is mutual authenticity that cements closeness. Of course, you need not reveal your entire life story prematurely. Start small: mention a challenge you are facing or an unusual hobby you love. If the group responds positively, you gain confidence in sharing more.

Acts of service within the tribe help cultivate belonging, too. Volunteer to coordinate an event, offer a helping hand if someone needs support, or bring snacks to a gathering. These gestures of contribution show that you care about the group's well-being. Others appreciate your involvement, seeing you as integral to the group's success. You move from a passive participant to an active collaborator. Over time, this involvement breeds recognition and mutual gratitude.

Celebrating milestones and successes strengthens belonging. When one member achieves something special, landing a new job, completing a creative project, acknowledge it as a collective triumph. Toast them at a meetup, post congratulations in your group chat, or give them a small keepsake. Such communal joy cements the idea that each individual's journey matters to everyone, forging emotional unity.

Respect for personal space ensures that belonging does not become smothering. Everyone needs the freedom to handle private matters or take breaks. Avoid pressuring someone who is not ready to open up fully or forcing them to join every gathering. Balancing inclusion with respect fosters a stable atmosphere. Each member senses they can be themselves, welcomed unconditionally without losing autonomy.

Finally, remember that belonging is a two-way street. If you notice someone in the group hanging back, gently draw them in. Ask for their viewpoint or give them a chance to share an idea. By including quieter members, you expand the sense of unity. That small gesture can encourage them to offer their unique insights, strengthening the group's collective wisdom.

Through consistent engagement, genuine sharing, communal support, and a relaxed respect for individuality, your sense of belonging within a tribe becomes increasingly tangible. In such a setting, you stop feeling like an outsider. Instead, you settle into a space that embraces who you are and celebrates your place in the wider circle. Over time, this sense of home expands beyond the group, enriching your overall perspective on community and interconnectedness.

The Healing Power of Tribal Support

Your tribe does more than offer companionship. When you endure personal crises or emotional wounds, your tribe can aid healing in ways no single professional or single friend alone might achieve. The collective warmth, empathy, and diverse set of experiences within a supportive group can provide multifaceted help. You sense you have a lifeline, a place where burdens can be shared and solutions mulled over in a safe environment.

The synergy of multiple supporters can be profound. One friend might lift your spirits with humour, while another brings thoughtful advice based on their past. A third may simply sit with you in silence, letting you vent without interruptions. Each individual brings a different resource. In the moments you feel battered by life, the breadth of compassion available can feel like stepping into a protective cocoon.

Emotional support aside, practical assistance also arises. If you are recovering from surgery, tribe members might coordinate meal deliveries or childcare. When you face job loss, they could tap into their networks or help polish your CV. This cooperative approach lessens the load, reminding you that you do not have to be solely responsible for solving every problem. Even small gestures, like running errands or sending encouraging texts, reinforce that you are cared for.

Belonging to a tribe also combats isolation. Emotional distress often comes with a sense of loneliness, as if you are the only one facing adversity. Hearing similar struggles from others normalises your experiences, diminishing shame or embarrassment. Perhaps a tribe member shares how they overcame depression or how they managed an ailing parent. Such stories carry healing power. They show resilience is possible and that it is all right to stumble. You become more hopeful about your own capacity to recover.

There can be spiritual or moral support, too, if your tribe shares a broader outlook on life. In times of grief or existential angst, words from a comforting perspective, whether rooted in faith or a simple universal compassion, offer solace. Rituals like group reflections, communal dinners, or heartfelt messages can comfort your inner spirit. These gestures remind you that life has meaning beyond your present suffering.

Furthermore, accountability from your tribe fosters longer-term healing. Once you begin to see daylight again, they might gently check in: "How's your therapy going?" or "Have you followed through on that self-care promise?" This accountability springs from a place of love, helping you maintain progress. Rather than feeling judged, you recognise they want you to remain healthy and stable. Their reassurance can prove critical when you are tempted to revert to harmful coping habits.

In a tumultuous world, the healing power of a supportive tribe is a beacon. They act as an emotional salve, a buffer against the harshness of life, and a guiding presence that buoys you. Over time, surviving hardships within a loving group fosters unshakeable bonds. Friends become akin to family, and the memory of their unwavering presence can shape your outlook, instilling gratitude and resilience. You realise that healing is not just an individual endeavour but also a collective triumph.

Evolving with Your Tribe

People grow, interests shift, and life circumstances change. The tribe you formed at one life stage may need to evolve to remain relevant and supportive. Perhaps members drift to new cities or adopt different lifestyles. Rather than seeing these changes as endings, look at them as transitions. A good tribe is malleable, capable of adapting while retaining the essence that brought you together in the first place.

An open dialogue about evolving needs is vital. If your group initially revolved around late-night socials, but half the members now have young children, everyone might find those gatherings too tiring. Reevaluating how and when you meet ensures the tribe does not fracture as personal obligations shift. Maybe you pivot to weekend brunches instead, or set up group messages that let parents with tight schedules remain connected.

New interests may arise. Suppose a few members of your tribe discover a fascination for hiking while others prefer indoor hobbies. Create sub-groups or rotating plans. No single activity must dominate every gathering. This fluid structure fosters inclusivity, letting members delve into pursuits that excite them. Evolving does not mean severing ties with those who do not share new interests; it means exploring ways to keep the tribe cohesive, even if not all attend every outing.

Another aspect is personal growth. Someone in the tribe might adopt new perspectives or embark on major changes, such as shifting career paths or grappling with new worldviews. Such transformations can challenge existing group dynamics. People who once saw eye to eye may now disagree. Communication and respect remain crucial: let them explain their new direction, be receptive, and see if the group can accommodate that diversity. Often, your tribe can expand in insight by integrating these fresh viewpoints, provided they do not conflict with core shared values.

Personal successes may strain relationships if envy creeps in or if the newly successful member's lifestyle drastically changes. A shift in financial status, for example, can affect how you meet or what you spend money on. Handling these scenarios with honesty is key: "I realise my situation has changed. How can we keep our gatherings comfortable for everyone?" By addressing it upfront, you reduce misunderstandings or silent resentments.

Maintaining an evolving tribe also requires letting go at times. If a member's values deviate to a degree that causes ongoing conflict or if they repeatedly undermine the group's harmony, parting ways might be necessary. Such a decision should not be taken lightly. Try open discussions first. If bridging the gap is not feasible, accept the transition gracefully. You can still wish them well. Not every relationship is meant to endure forever; the tribe can remain strong if it is grounded in authenticity.

Finally, welcome new additions if they resonate with the group's spirit. A friend might bring someone who shares similar values. Integrating them can rejuvenate the dynamic, introducing fresh ideas and fostering deeper community. Over time, this constant ebb and flow ensures the tribe remains vibrant, reflecting the evolving tapestry of its members. By allowing for growth and change, your group matures, preserving the essence of connection while adapting to each new chapter in members' lives.

In Conclusion

You have delved into the idea of seeking and maintaining your tribe, people bound to you by more than mere acquaintance. You learned that shared values, mutual respect, and adaptability underpin a robust sense of belonging. Your tribe fosters support, understanding, and growth, becoming a sturdy anchor in both calm waters and storms.

In the upcoming chapters, you will revisit connections closer to home, examining how family dynamics shape your bonds and how you can nurture them into more positive experiences. Continue with an open heart, remembering the lessons gained: that relationships flourish when you share genuine understanding and a willingness to adapt. This mindset paves the way for more cohesive, supportive networks across all areas of your life.

Chapter 5

The Art of Connection in Family Dynamics

You may have spent your life building countless relationships, yet family connections often carry the most weight. From birth, you are shaped by family patterns, both positive and negative. This chapter explores how to strengthen these foundational ties so they serve as a source of mutual love rather than lingering tension. Family can bring comfort, but it can also harbour old wounds that need healing. The aim here is to highlight how you can cultivate a healthier, more compassionate dynamic, starting with your immediate family and extending to relatives you see less often.

You will find a blend of deep insights and practical steps, from understanding the energy that flows within a family to addressing childhood hurts that still affect you today. No matter whether your family is close-knit or spread across different corners of the world, this chapter will guide you in relating to them with renewed empathy and purpose. Ultimately, it is about transforming the family unit into one that nurtures each member. As you turn these pages, get ready to explore a more uplifting, balanced way of interacting with loved ones, one that endures through life's inevitable ups and downs.

Understanding Family Energy Dynamics

Connections

Families may share many things, from physical features to longstanding traditions, but an often overlooked element is the energy that each person brings to the collective environment. You can sense it when you enter your parents' home or attend a cousin's gathering: the emotional tone feels charged, whether with warmth, tension, or a mix of both. Becoming aware of this invisible layer is the first step toward fostering better connections. In family units, energy tends to circulate in a loop. If one member is upset or stressed, the ripple can move quickly to others, who might respond in frustration or withdrawal. Alternatively, if someone is calm and supportive, they may defuse tension and encourage more open, productive discussions. In this way, each member's emotional state can shift the entire group dynamic. By recognising these undercurrents, you gain the power to guide interactions more positively.

Your childhood might also have laid the foundation for how you manage and express energy within the family. If conflicts were handled through loud arguments, you may have absorbed the idea that speaking louder wins the day. On the other hand, if problems were swept under the rug, you could be prone to silent resentment. These ingrained tendencies continue to shape family interactions into adulthood. The key is to notice these patterns without self-blame, then make conscious changes that allow for better communication.

Being mindful of triggers helps you navigate potential conflicts. Think about the topics or behaviours that spark strong emotional responses, such as discussing finances, certain life choices, or unresolved feuds. Once aware, you can plan how to respond calmly instead of falling into knee-jerk reactions. For example, if a sibling consistently criticises your career path, you might adopt a script in your mind to keep the conversation neutral. By preparing emotionally, you avoid letting their negativity permeate your own mood.

Boundaries are equally important in family energy dynamics. While family members might feel they can comment on every aspect of your life, you are free to establish limits. If an aunt probes about your personal affairs that you prefer not to share, respond politely but succinctly. Over time, gently repeating these limits teaches them where your boundaries lie. By protecting your emotional space, you maintain control over how much influence others' energies hold.

Technology can also influence family energy. Quick exchanges in group chats, if written hastily, can be misread as hostile. Misunderstandings multiply when people interpret short answers as dismissive. If emotions escalate, remind yourself that tone is easily lost in digital text. Suggest a quick phone call or a face-to-face meeting to clear up confusion. Such deliberate approaches often preserve harmony that otherwise gets derailed by ambiguous messages.

Learning to channel family energy effectively does not mean turning into a detached observer. It means leading by example, practising empathy, listening actively, and sharing your own feelings with honesty. When you see tension rising, step up as a stabilising force. Your measured responses can inspire others to mirror your calm, thereby diffusing group stress. Ultimately, your personal shifts can create a ripple effect, easing old conflicts and encouraging a more balanced, supportive atmosphere for everyone involved.

Healing Familial Wounds

Family wounds can cut deep, often leaving you with lingering discomfort even when you grow into adulthood. These might be based on hurtful remarks, broken trust, or actions taken during times of stress or emotional volatility. Though part of you might yearn to leave the past behind, unresolved pain can quietly colour your present connections. Healing becomes essential for moving forward.

To start, allow yourself to acknowledge any residual hurt. It may feel tempting to bury old grievances, particularly if your family never openly discusses problems. But repressed feelings rarely vanish. They tend to manifest in subtle ways: anxiety at family gatherings, difficulty trusting relatives, or hostility that flares up unexpectedly. Admission that a painful experience occurred, even if it was in childhood, can be a vital step. You could journal about it or talk privately to a trusted friend, giving yourself permission to feel.

After naming the wound, reflection and perspective-taking can help you see it in a broader context. This does not minimise what happened, but it can offer insights into why your relative acted in that way. Perhaps your mother was under severe financial stress, or your father battled personal demons. While understanding does not excuse harmful behaviour, it can alleviate some emotional heaviness, allowing you to differentiate the act from malicious intent. This mindset shift can gently open the door to forgiveness if it feels appropriate.

Sometimes, direct communication helps. If the person who caused the hurt is willing to listen, attempt an honest conversation. Approach it calmly. State the facts of what happened and how it impacted you, focusing on your

The Art of Connection in Family Dynamics

feelings rather than blaming them. For instance, "When you said those things about my choices, I felt crushed because your opinion matters to me." This approach seeks mutual understanding rather than retribution. They might respond with regret, or they may be defensive. Either way, you have voiced your perspective, which can be liberating by itself.

Therapy or counselling offers another pathway for healing, especially if the wound is embedded deeply. A professional can guide you in processing emotions and learning coping tools. Family therapy might be an option if multiple members are open to it. If your sibling or parent is truly remorseful, guided sessions can pave the way for honest apologies and new beginnings. Keep in mind that healing does not require the entire family to cooperate. Even solitary therapy can free you from the weight of old pain.

Patience is crucial. Healing rarely happens overnight. You may make strides toward calm acceptance, only to feel old hurts resurface during a heated family gathering. Do not interpret this as failure. Each step forward, however small, is progress. You build emotional resilience by repeatedly choosing to address your pain rather than let it dictate your interactions. Over time, you find that the sting of old wounds lessens and is replaced by a sense of closure.

Finally, actively seek hope in your relationships. Even if certain dynamics remain difficult, focus on moments of warmth or kindness. These do not erase the past but can balance your perspective. You remind yourself that people can evolve, and relationships can shift in positive ways. With the clarity gained through healing, you become more inclined to foster constructive communication. In this sense, repairing family wounds is not solely about dwelling on yesteryear's sorrows. It is about creating an environment where current and future generations can relate in a healthier, more uplifting manner.

Building Bridges: Improving Family Connections

Families can become fragmented through misunderstandings, distance, or sheer busyness. Bridging these gaps takes intentional effort, but the results can be transformative. You do not want to let time slip away without forging closer bonds, particularly with those who share a large segment of your life story. By taking proactive steps, you can strengthen communication and bring greater harmony to these fundamental relationships.

One effective starting point is scheduling regular interactions that go beyond obligatory gatherings. If family members live nearby, organise monthly meals or casual get-togethers. Even if you have daily tasks, an hour or two spent having quality conversation can work wonders. If relatives live far away, organise video calls. The key is to have a consistent plan. This consistency reminds everyone that family connection matters enough to reserve time in your busy schedule.

During these shared moments, aim to move conversations beyond the superficial. Ask open-ended questions that spark deeper discussion: "What has challenged you lately?", "What are you excited about next month?" or "How can we support each other better?" Such prompts encourage honesty and vulnerability. If a relative seems hesitant, be patient and lead by example. When they see your sincere willingness to share parts of your life, they may feel safer to open up about their experiences.

The Art of Connection in Family Dynamics

Be sure to celebrate small achievements. If your sibling mentions finishing a personal project or a new hobby, acknowledge it enthusiastically. Family members often yearn for validation and understanding from their kin. By offering recognition and cheering them on, you show that you genuinely care. These affirmations can deepen the bond, turning mere acquaintanceship into real companionship. Moreover, they counterbalance any negativity that might arise from past tensions.

Focusing on collaboration also fortifies connections. Whether planning a holiday meal or tackling a family property issue, approach tasks as a team. Involve everyone in decision-making, letting each person's voice be heard. Delegating roles fosters a shared sense of purpose. If opinions clash, calm negotiations highlight respect. You might say, "I understand you want this method; can we explore both approaches to see what fits best?" This approach can transform potentially divisive tasks into cooperative experiences.

It is also helpful to keep communication channels open between larger family events. Send messages out of genuine interest: "I am thinking of you; how has your week been?" or forward an article that resonates with a topic you once discussed. This demonstrates that you remember details from your chats and that your concern does not vanish when you part ways. A small note or quick phone call can be enough to remind them you are there, bridging the distance that daily life otherwise creates.

Lastly, always approach bridging efforts with realistic expectations. You might desire immediate warmth and togetherness, but some family dynamics take time to thaw.

If unresolved tension or old resentments linger, your consistent show of goodwill might slowly encourage others to respond in kind. Let small improvements accumulate. Each positive encounter fosters trust, inching you closer toward the supportive family framework you envision. With persistence, you will likely witness the strengthening of relationships that once felt strained or dormant, paving a brighter path for future gatherings and overall unity.

The Role of Unconditional Love in Family

Unconditional love is often described as love that stands firm regardless of flaws or mistakes. In a family setting, it forms the backbone of emotional security. You can grow up feeling safe when you know that, despite arguments or setbacks, your relatives still welcome you. However, unconditional love does not remove personal responsibility or boundaries. Instead, it offers a foundation where your worth is never questioned, even when conflicts arise.

To foster unconditional love, start by recognising that each family member is more than their shortcomings. Perhaps your sibling can be impatient, or your uncle is overly critical. Yes, these traits can be frustrating, but unconditional love looks beyond them. It acknowledges that people act from complex motives shaped by past pains, insecurities, or stress. When you remember these layers, empathy becomes easier. This empathy is not about excusing poor behaviour but about holding a broader perspective: "This person is flawed, as am I, but we remain bonded by something deeper."

Words of affirmation are a simple yet powerful demonstration of unconditional love. You might say, "I cherish who you are," or "I care about you, no matter what you are facing." Even when offering constructive feedback, centre it in love: "I disagree with your decision here, but my support for you stands." These clarifications help family members feel secure, reminding them that disagreement is not rejection. Over time, such statements normalise the idea that mistakes or differences do not sever the family bond.

Consistency is crucial. If you proclaim unconditional love but constantly threaten to withdraw it unless family members conform to your wishes, it contradicts the principle. Real unconditional love means continuing to treat them with dignity, even when you are upset or disappointed. However, you can still maintain boundaries. You might say, "I care deeply, but I cannot accept harmful actions." This approach teaches respect without jeopardising the underlying affection you hold.

Within this framework, forgiveness becomes more accessible. People do wrong one another, sometimes inadvertently. When unconditional love is present, the path to reconciliation is smoother. You already hold the awareness that your affection for them endures beyond their slip-up. As a result, apologising and forgiving can happen more swiftly. Mistakes are approached as events to learn from rather than reasons to disconnect permanently.

Unconditional love also requires self-compassion. If you can accept your own imperfections, you are more likely to extend similar grace to others. When you find yourself seething at a parent's or child's repeated failures, pause to recall times when you felt limited by your own flaws. This reflection can soften your stance, enabling you to respond with understanding rather than anger. By modelling this behaviour, you demonstrate to others that unconditional love is possible, even in challenging circumstances.

A final thought on unconditional love involves resilience. Families go through tests, from financial crises to emotional heartbreaks. The knowledge that you are loved wholly becomes a buffer against despair. It reassures you that if you falter or make a regrettable choice, you still have a place to call home. In that sense, unconditional love is more than a comforting phrase; it is an active, persistent effort that anchors the family in genuine unity, bridging differences and fostering lifelong loyalty.

Navigating Family Conflicts with Empathy

Conflict is inevitable in any close relationship, but family conflicts often feel especially intense due to deep emotional history. You might feel instantly triggered by a sibling's remarks or a parent's criticism, as it connects to old insecurities. Yet empathy can be your greatest ally, transforming heated arguments into constructive dialogues. While empathy does not mean agreeing with everything a relative says, it involves seeking to understand their perspective on a human level.

When a dispute arises, pause your urge to respond immediately. You can take a breath, ground yourself, and reflect on what might be driving the other person's frustration. Are they anxious because they fear losing something they value? Has a recent event upset them, and your comment merely set off an underlying worry? Pondering these questions shifts your focus from defending yourself to exploring the root of the conflict, helping you approach them with compassion.

The Art of Connection in Family Dynamics

Mindful listening also matters. Let them speak without jumping in, using nods or short affirmations to indicate you hear them. If your parent is angry over your life choices, for example, say: "I see that you are worried about my decisions." Summarising their points helps them feel validated. This does not signify you agree, but it reassures them that you are taking their viewpoint seriously, which often reduces hostility. Once they feel heard, they may become more open to your explanation.

As you respond, avoid blaming language. State your position using "I" statements, such as, "I felt unheard when you brushed aside my concerns," or "I am trying to follow my path, and I value your guidance, but I need room to decide." This framing emphasises your emotions rather than attacking their character. It also opens the door for them to respond without feeling cornered, which can lessen defensive reactions.

Empathy can extend to your own feelings, too. If you are emotionally raw, show kindness to yourself. Take a break if the argument becomes too heated: "I need a moment to think. Let us continue this in a calmer state." This short pause can be valuable; you both get space to calm down, preventing the conflict from escalating with words you might regret. After a breather, you may return with a cooler head, more able to empathise instead of reacting from hurt or pride.

Sometimes an impartial mediator may help if tensions remain high. That might be a relative who is not directly involved in the issue, or even a professional counsellor. A neutral voice can clarify misunderstandings or break down communication barriers, ensuring that empathy remains central in the resolution process. Such structured discussions can lead to breakthroughs, allowing pent-up emotions to be aired in a guided, respectful environment.

Finally, remember that empathy-driven conflicts do not always end in full agreement. The real aim is not victory but mutual understanding and respect. You might leave the table with differences intact but also with a sense of deeper insight into one another's motivations. Over time, practising empathetic conflict management can reshape family patterns. You prove that disagreements approached thoughtfully, can lead to learning and unity rather than division. The atmosphere becomes calmer, and trust builds when relatives see you choose empathy rather than hostility, forging a more harmonious family dynamic.

Setting Healthy Boundaries in Family Relationships

When it comes to family, setting boundaries is one of the trickiest tasks. You may have been raised to prioritise familial expectations over personal well-being, leaving you feeling obliged to comply with every request. Though loyalty is important, letting relatives intrude on your emotional space or personal choices can lead to resentment. Healthy boundaries ensure you remain supportive while safeguarding your mental health.

Begin by identifying areas where you feel stretched. This might involve repeated phone calls asking for immediate help or criticism about personal matters like career or parenting decisions. Once you notice these patterns, clarify for yourself what you do and do not find acceptable. For instance, if your parent frequently comments on your weight or lifestyle, you can decide that such commentary is off-limits in conversations. Articulating it to yourself first helps you communicate it more confidently later.

Communicating boundaries requires tact. If your sibling assumes you are available at all hours, politely mention that you cannot answer calls after a certain time. By stating it calmly and holding firm, you shape new expectations. Avoid lengthy justifications, as that can invite debates about your choices. A concise explanation, "I am focusing on rest, so I will be turning my phone off after 9pm," is enough. Although they might feel surprised initially, consistent reinforcement will help them adapt.

Another scenario is when relatives directly invade your privacy. Perhaps they pressure you about personal relationships or finances. In these instances, respond gently but be firm. "I appreciate your concern, but I prefer not to discuss that right now," or "I am handling it privately." Refrain from giving ambiguous answers that leave room for more probing. Stick to your line and pivot the conversation to a more comfortable topic. Over time, family members often learn to respect these limits.

Of course, tension might arise, particularly if some relatives dislike boundaries. They could interpret your stance as rejection or become defensive, claiming, "We are family, so we talk about everything." Reassure them you still care, but you have the right to shape what you share. For instance, "I value our bond, but discussing my personal finances is something I am not comfortable with. Let us focus on other updates in our lives." This approach emphasises that you still value the relationship, even as you maintain a boundary around sensitive matters.

Boundaries also extend to emotional labour. If a relative constantly unloads their woes without considering your capacity to listen, it is fair to say, "I am sorry you are having a hard time; I have some pressing tasks and cannot talk more about it now." This balanced tone offers empathy without allowing yourself to be consumed by someone else's issues. By practising this, you show that your support has limits, preventing burnout.

Boundaries are not about pushing family away but about structuring respectful engagement. When you draw the lines consistently and kindly, relatives often adjust. Ultimately, these protective measures let you invest in relationships in a healthy manner, preventing bitterness or disconnection. Over time, everyone benefits from a climate of mutual respect, ensuring that family ties remain sources of comfort rather than distress.

The Impact of Family History on Your Energy

Family history is woven into your identity more deeply than you might realise. From traditions to inherited mannerisms, you carry echoes of past generations. This legacy can be enriching, but it can also harbour baggage that weighs on your psyche. Whether it is old trauma, unspoken resentments, or cultural expectations passed down over decades, these ancestral threads can shape how you handle conflict, nurture relationships, or see yourself.

Early memories often reveal how these influences took hold. Perhaps you recall observing how your grandparents tackled disagreements or how older siblings acted when finances were tight. Unconsciously, these impressions become internal scripts. If your family typically avoided open discussions, you might sense anxiety whenever you need to address an issue. If they believed in stoic independence, you might struggle to ask for help, even when you genuinely need it. Recognising these patterns is the first step in freeing yourself from unhelpful legacies.

Another layer is the beliefs about success, marriage, or lifestyle that your family imparts. For instance, a lineage of entrepreneurs may instil you with a do-it-yourself spirit, but also an aversion to steady employment. Or a background of stable public service roles might make you fear venturing into uncertain territory. By reflecting on these influences, you can decide which inherited beliefs serve you and which hamper your growth. In doing so, you separate your authentic desires from automatic family conditioning.

Emotional patterns also carry forward. If your family seldom showed affection, you may find it awkward to hug relatives, even when you crave warmth. Or if older generations were quick to judge, you might adopt a hypercritical stance toward yourself and others. None of these patterns are unchangeable. By acknowledging them, you empower yourself to adapt. You can decide, "Yes, my background was like that, but I choose a different way."

Healing generational wounds often requires deeper exploration. Some families experience a cycle of destructive behaviour, such as addictions or controlling tendencies. In these cases, a multigenerational perspective can be revealing. For example, if your grandparents faced severe hardships and developed survival mechanisms, these might have trickled down as overly strict parenting in your own family. Understanding these origins fosters empathy. You see your relatives not as villains but as people shaped by their times. Still, you can choose to break the cycle by adopting healthier strategies for dealing with stress or raising children.

Family gatherings might spark triggers related to this inherited energy. A seemingly harmless comment from an older aunt can stir complicated emotions rooted in your youth. Being mindful of these triggers helps you respond calmly. Instead of acting purely on old reflexes, you can say, "I see where this discomfort comes from. I am no longer a child bound by those past dynamics." This self-talk is a way to rewire your emotional responses.

Ultimately, acknowledging family history does not mean you are condemned to repeat it. On the contrary, awareness grants you the power to filter out negative legacies while keeping what enriches your life. Learning how your ancestors coped, loved, or endured adversity can be a source of inspiration. By harnessing the positive strands and consciously discarding harmful ones, you shape your own identity. You stand rooted in your heritage, yet free to define your path on your own terms.

Forgiving and Letting Go of Past Hurts

Forgiveness within a family context can be both liberating and complicated. You might feel deeply wronged by relatives or upset about events that occurred decades ago. Over time, resentments harden into barriers that spoil the atmosphere whenever you gather. Yet, holding on to that anger keeps you chained to old pain. Letting go is a personal choice that frees you from emotional burdens, though it is vital to understand what forgiveness truly means.

Forgiveness is not the same as blindly trusting someone who has hurt you. Nor does it require you to condone harmful actions or pretend the past never happened. Instead, it

The Art of Connection in Family Dynamics

involves releasing the heavy load of bitterness you carry. You choose not to let that resentment dominate your current life. Doing so can lessen anxiety or emotional triggers, granting you a sense of peace. At times, you might still keep boundaries, particularly if a family member's behaviour remains problematic.

To begin, acknowledge the pain. You cannot forgive what you do not admit. Write down what transpired and how it affected you, whether it is a parent who was absent or a sibling who betrayed your trust. Identify the emotions attached: anger, betrayal, sadness, or confusion. This clarity helps you address the hurt. Masking it under a forced smile or waiting for time to erase it rarely leads to real resolution.

Next, reflect on how continuing anger serves you. While it might give a sense of moral high ground or partial control, it also drains your vitality. Each time you recall that incident, you relive negative emotions. Forgiveness, ironically, does more for your own mental health than for the person you forgive. It breaks the chain that ties you to harmful experiences, allowing you to invest your energy in healthier pursuits.

Communication can aid this process, though it is not always mandatory. If the other party is open, share your desire to move on. You might say, "I have been hurt by what happened, but I am willing to release this anger." They may apologise or defend themselves. If they offer genuine remorse, it can help you both heal. If not, your forgiveness remains a personal path. You are not dependent on their response; you can still choose to let go for your own peace.

At times, a formal gesture helps. Some find it therapeutic to write a letter detailing the hurt and concluding with an affirmation of forgiveness, then destroying it or storing it out of sight. The physical act can symbolise closure. Alternatively, speak to a counsellor or someone you trust, articulating your readiness to move forward. This step transforms an internal decision into a tangible milestone, anchoring your commitment to release the pain.

Finally, practise patience with yourself. Old wounds can linger, and feelings might resurface occasionally. Forgiving once does not guarantee you will never feel upset again. Whenever anger creeps back, remind yourself of your choice. Acknowledge that you are still healing and reaffirm your decision to avoid allowing resentment to dominate. Over time, you will find the sting of past hurts softens. You reclaim the emotional space once taken up by negative memories, leaving room for more constructive interactions and a deeper sense of peace with your family.

The Power of Family Rituals and Traditions

Rituals and traditions serve as anchors in family life, providing structure and continuity. Whether you share a regular Sunday lunch, gather during celebrations, or partake in an annual tradition, these shared events pull everyone out of their individual concerns for a while, focusing attention on collective harmony. Such rituals often evoke childhood nostalgia and keep cultural or familial identity alive. Beyond nostalgia, they can have a unifying impact, helping you reconnect with relatives you rarely see.

A well-loved tradition might be as straightforward as preparing a festive meal together. Each person has a role: an aunt might handle the main course while you whip up a dessert. The synergy of collective effort fosters teamwork,

The Art of Connection in Family Dynamics

and the meal feels far more meaningful than if you all ate separately. Plus, the repeated practice allows new members, like in-laws or younger cousins, to join in, bridging generational gaps.

Rituals need not be grand. A simple tradition, such as an evening board game, can bring siblings back into the same room, laughing and debating strategy. If everyone is scattered geographically, you can create digital traditions, like a monthly video call. Perhaps you all enjoy telling funny anecdotes from your childhood or showcasing new skills. Even if it seems small, consistency cements the bond. It reminds you that family is not just about shared bloodline but shared experiences.

Traditions also help pass down values. If your family always volunteers at a local event each autumn, younger members observe altruism in action. If your family is known for preserving a local craft, teaching the technique to each new generation ensures that skill does not fade. Through these shared activities, you demonstrate your collective identity. You do not need lengthy lectures if your entire clan demonstrates these core principles by living them out in each tradition.

New beginnings can also be turned into rituals. For instance, if a family member graduates, you might organise an annual recognition dinner for educational achievements. Or if someone moves into a new home, you all gather to help with painting or repairs. Over the years, these recurring gestures weave a deeper sense of loyalty. They say, "We are here for each other in both joyous and challenging transitions." The repetition of these events fosters a comforting predictability, giving every member something to look forward to.

Change, however, can disrupt traditions. As relatives relocate or pass away, you might lose a key figure who always led a holiday ceremony. Instead of letting that tradition vanish, find a way to honour their contribution while adapting the practice. This might be as simple as telling a beloved story that reminds everyone of their role or adding new elements that reflect the current family's needs. By embracing evolution, you keep traditions alive and relevant without discarding their emotional value.

Ultimately, rituals and traditions serve as a family's connective tissue, bridging generational gaps and fuelling collective identity. They provide a stable rhythm amidst life's uncertainties, reminding everyone that beyond daily stresses, there is a supportive circle bound by recurring customs. Whether it is a group prayer, a big dinner, or a playful competition, these shared moments can become cherished memories. They fortify your sense of belonging, passing from one generation to the next as a living inheritance of unity and warmth.

Reinforcing Positive Connections within the Family

Maintaining positivity in family bonds is a continual practice, not a one-off achievement. Even if your family has made strides toward better communication and mutual understanding, daily life can bring fresh challenges that threaten to unravel hard-won harmony. It is through consistent effort and a mindful approach that you keep the spirit of unity strong.

One way to reinforce positive ties is by voicing appreciation often. You might say, "Thank you for always being supportive," or "I admire how you handled that situation at

The Art of Connection in Family Dynamics

work." These gestures remind each family member they are valued, counteracting the negativity that sometimes arises in close quarters. Routine appreciation counterbalances small irritations and missteps, preventing them from overshadowing the goodwill that you have built.

Encourage each other's personal growth. When a sibling embarks on a new career path, a spouse chooses to learn a skill, or a parent tries a fresh hobby, cheer them on. Listen to their updates or progress. Ask them about any challenges. Your curiosity and encouragement fuel their motivation to keep going. In turn, this fosters an environment of mutual empowerment. Each success or milestone becomes a shared victory, enriching the family's collective spirit.

Another helpful approach is to check in proactively rather than waiting for problems to escalate. For instance, if you sense tension in a parent's voice or see signs of stress in a partner, gently ask how they are feeling. Doing so can uncover issues before they balloon. A short, mindful conversation might prevent misunderstandings from festering. Over time, consistent check-ins build trust, signalling that you are present not merely for major events but also for everyday concerns.

You also strengthen familial bonds by creating memories beyond obligations. Holidays tend to be emotional flashpoints, but what about smaller gatherings or spontaneous meetups? Plan a casual day trip with your immediate family or invite cousins for an informal barbeque. Laughter and shared experiences during these relaxed occasions can hold more emotional weight than formal gatherings, occasionally overshadowed by stress. The more pleasant memories you create together, the more resilient you become when friction arises.

Finally, keep evolving in how you address conflicts. Family members grow and change, so a method that resolved past quarrels may not apply to new ones. Perhaps your sibling once needed a gentle approach, but now they prefer direct feedback, or vice versa. Remain flexible. Frequently revisit the question of what each person finds helpful in resolving disagreements. You might discover that collective problem-solving sessions or short, private discussions are more effective than large family interventions. The aim is to fine-tune your strategies so that no one feels overwhelmed, sidelined, or invalidated.

When you put these behaviours into regular practice, you reinforce positivity in a lasting way. You show that you are committed to fostering unity, not just smoothing over a one-time issue. This creates a solid foundation for the entire family, preventing minor hiccups from turning into lasting rifts. A family that routinely communicates, celebrates each other's growth, and respects boundaries stands a better chance of thriving despite life's inevitable trials.

In Conclusion

In this chapter, you explored the many facets of family life, from hidden energy patterns to rituals that bond relatives. You have seen that creating a loving household involves understanding family history, establishing boundaries, and choosing forgiveness. By putting these steps into practice, you strengthen the core relationships that define your earliest sense of belonging.

The Art of Connection in Family Dynamics

Next, you will discover the wide realm of friendship, another vital network for emotional support and companionship. You will learn how these chosen bonds can enrich your journey, offering a space to grow and share life's joys, distinct from but equally as nourishing as family ties. Let us now step outside the family circle and look at how to create and maintain fulfilling friendships.

Chapter 6

Friendship: The Bonds That Sustain Us

While family shapes your early emotional experiences, friendships often guide your journey through life's transitions. You gravitate to friends who share your interests, understand your quirks, and offer understanding without judgement. As an adult, friendships become a crucial sanctuary for personal growth and joy. Yet, they also require nurturing, effort, and resilience. This chapter explores the changing dynamics of friendship and how you can maintain deep connections despite new responsibilities and life phases.

Here, you will unpack the nature of adult friendship. You will learn about sustaining bonds through major life changes, whether that is a career shift, marriage, or relocation. You will see how to handle betrayals, deepen the relationships you already have, and know when it is kinder to let go. As you reflect on these pages, you will gain insights that help you craft the enduring friendships you deserve, ones that support you in becoming your best self at every milestone.

The Evolution of Friendship in Adult Life

Childhood friendships often begin out of convenience, proximity, or shared classrooms. In youth, you may spend hours playing games, exploring neighbourhoods, or simply bonding over silly jokes. With adulthood, friendships transform. While you once had an abundance of free time to engage in carefree pursuits, adult responsibilities shift priorities, and the way you build or sustain friendships must adapt.

Your late teens might have introduced you to a broader social scene, such as university or early employment, where forging new bonds felt thrilling. As you move further into adulthood, many relationships revolve around shared life stages: colleagues who empathise with your work environment, other parents you meet through children's activities, or people you encounter in community events relevant to your interests. This transition to adulthood often underlines the importance of quality over quantity. You can no longer hang out aimlessly for hours, so you value deeper conversations that enrich your limited spare time.

Career paths also shape the way you engage socially. Working full-time can hamper your ability to see old friends. You might move to a new region, leaving behind childhood pals, or the demands of a high-pressure job may reduce your social life to weekends. This can lead to a sense of loss for the easier connectivity of youth, but it also sparks creativity in how you keep in touch. You might set up monthly group calls or plan an annual gathering with your long-term mates. Such deliberate planning keeps bonds alive when spontaneous get-togethers become scarce.

Another layer of complexity arises when your life differs significantly from that of a friend. One might marry and start a family early, while the other travels extensively or prioritises career goals. Both paths are valid, but they can limit common ground. Friendship does not require matching life choices, though. If you remain open-minded and respectful, these differences can broaden your outlook. You adapt to fresh perspectives. Perhaps you gain admiration for a friend's busy parenthood schedule, or they appreciate your adventurous spirit. By acknowledging each other's lifestyles, you preserve connections that might otherwise fizzle.

Friendships also evolve in how conflicts are handled. In childhood, an argument might mean refusing to share toys for an afternoon. As adults, disputes can be more nuanced, involving deeper emotions or bigger consequences. Mending the rifts may require honest dialogue rather than simply waiting for them to pass. You see that a single conversation can restore the bond, provided both sides are willing to listen and compromise.

Lastly, as you accumulate adult experiences, your perspective on loyalty, boundaries, and what you need from a friend becomes clearer. You no longer have endless capacity for shallow or drama-filled connections. Instead, you lean towards those who offer mutual respect, empathy, and constructive support. This selective approach can feel bittersweet. You might leave behind some old circles, but the resulting friendships are more authentic and aligned with your adult values. Embracing these evolutions helps you maintain rich relationships that uplift you through the varied stages of adulthood.

Qualities of Enduring Friendships

When you look at friendships that last for years, certain core attributes stand out. They are not built solely on liking the same activities or having a similar background. Rather, enduring bonds rely on deeper qualities such as trust, empathy, and reciprocal support. By focusing on these aspects, you can cultivate relationships that remain solid through life's changing tides.

Trust is primary. Over time, you confide in friends about vulnerabilities, from personal fears to private dreams. The safety you feel in sharing stems from trusting them not to belittle or betray you. When a friend proves they handle your secrets with care, that bond gains strength. Trust is also about reliability. If they promise to show up or help in a particular way, you sense they will follow through. This reliability fosters emotional security, letting you open up even more.

Another key is respect for individuality. True friends do not push you to be someone you are not. They value your quirks, even if they do not share your passions. Perhaps you love reading historical accounts, while they prefer action movies, yet they respect your tastes and show interest. You, in turn, do the same for them. This mutual acceptance means neither has to pretend or suppress who they are. Over years, as each person grows or changes direction, that respect remains the glue that keeps you connected.

Empathy also figures prominently. When you go through tough times, an enduring friend does not dismiss your feelings or skip straight to generic advice. They genuinely try to understand your perspective. This might involve listening quietly as you vent or offering gentle words that acknowledge the difficulty you face. You do the same for them when they need a shoulder. This cycle of empathetic listening builds closeness that can survive challenges or disagreements.

Shared experiences do contribute to the bond, but these experiences can be mental as well as physical. Holding a deep conversation over a cup of tea can be just as bonding as a holiday together. The underlying factor is genuine interaction. Are you exchanging thoughts and truly hearing each other's stories or merely passing time with small talk? Enduring friends often find they can pick up right where they left off, even if they have not spoken for months, because their emotional connection is grounded in sincerity, not superficiality.

Conflict resolution skills further set enduring friendships apart. Inevitably, you might say something hurtful or fail to be there at a key moment. A lasting friend addresses the issue instead of letting resentment grow. They approach conflicts with honesty and a spirit of reconciliation, trusting you will do the same. Forgiveness is central here. Both of you acknowledge mistakes, apologise where needed, and move forward stronger than before. This capacity to repair rifts is vital for long-term closeness.

Finally, an important but overlooked quality is genuine happiness for each other's success. Some friendships strain under jealousy if one person experiences major achievements. In robust friendships, your triumphs delight your friend, and you feel the same about their victories. There is no competition, only celebration. This positive energy fosters an environment that nurtures both parties' self-confidence, making the bond an uplifting force. When you find these attributes in a friend, you know you can journey through life's unpredictable paths together, standing firm through all seasons.

Navigating Seasons of Change in Friendships

Change is a constant in life, and your friendships are not exempt. Whether it is a shift in career, moving to a different area, getting married, or starting a family, transitions can alter how you relate to your friends. While you may fear that a big change means losing people you love, it can also serve as a catalyst for exploring new ways to keep those bonds alive.

One major element is communication. If your routine changes because of a new job with demanding hours, let your friends know in advance. Say, "My schedule is hectic for the next few months; it might be harder to catch me spontaneously, but I still want to stay connected." By spelling out the shift, you pre-empt misunderstandings if you become less available. They are likely to respect your honesty and adapt accordingly.

Sometimes, life events lead you in separate directions. One friend might travel abroad for a year; another might start an intensive course that leaves little room for socialising. You can see the reduction in face-to-face time as a potential wedge, but with a bit of creativity, you can remain close. A monthly video call or a consistent messaging routine helps maintain the sense of intimacy. As you each share stories, from thrilling adventures to mundane day-to-day details, the gap in physical presence is bridged by emotional closeness.

Accept that certain friendships are situational, thriving in one chapter but diminishing in another. This is not necessarily a bad outcome. If you look back at your childhood or university days, you may recall dear friends with whom you have since lost touch. Sometimes, that occurs naturally as you both evolve and find different pursuits. If you wish to preserve such connections, you must invest energy. But if repeated attempts to reconnect stall, it might suggest that you have both moved on. Instead of seeing it as a failure, recall the good you shared during that season and hold gratitude for the time you had.

Maintain realistic expectations. The friend who was your closest confidant when you lived on the same street might now be busy raising a family. Their capacity to talk at length could be limited. Meanwhile, you might have discovered new interests that they do not share. A friendship can still endure if you accept these changes. Focus on the aspects you still have in common, plan time that fits both your schedules, or alternate who hosts visits. This mutual flexibility keeps the link strong, reminding you that the foundation of a solid bond can surpass logistical hurdles.

Another factor is personal growth. As you or your friend work on self-improvement, your values and perspectives may shift. Sometimes, this draws you closer, while in other cases, the gap widens. A supportive approach is key here. If you sense differences forming, talk about them openly. Ask your friend about their new insights, and share yours. Such discussions can lead to a richer bond, provided you both remain open-minded.

In essence, navigating changing seasons means staying proactive, communicative, and open to adjustment. Rather than resisting the natural ebb and flow, embrace it. Appreciate that your friend's place in your life may shift, but with deliberate care, you can preserve the essence of your bond. This approach fosters resilience, proving that with the right balance of effort and acceptance, your friendship can flourish over many chapters of your life story.

The Impact of Social Media on Real Connections

Friendship: The Bonds That Sustain Us

Social media platforms have revolutionised how you keep up with your friends, but they also present new challenges to forming deeper connections. On one hand, you can reconnect with acquaintances from your school days or stay in touch with a cousin living overseas. Regular updates give you a glimpse into each other's lives, fostering familiarity that might otherwise fade with distance. Yet behind these conveniences lurk pitfalls that can affect the quality of your friendships.

One common issue is the curated nature of social media. Friends often post their happiest experiences or major achievements, giving an impression of unceasing success or cheer. This can trigger comparisons, prompting you to feel inadequate if your real day-to-day is fraught with challenges. It also creates a somewhat shallow sense of knowing what is happening in a friend's life. Clicking "like" on a holiday photo does not compare to a genuine conversation about their joys and worries.

Additionally, rapid or superficial interactions can dull the drive for meaningful chats. When you see a friend's status updates daily, you might assume you know how they are doing without actually talking to them. Over time, the friendship can weaken if you rely on these second-hand glimpses rather than direct engagement. Real friendships thrive on deeper dialogue and empathy, elements often lacking in short social media comments or emojis.

On the flip side, social media can be a stepping stone for in-person meetups. If you notice a friend is local or shares your interest in a new hobby, send a private message suggesting a coffee. Digital contact can morph into real-life bonding if used as a starting point instead of an end. This tactic is especially helpful if you are in a new area and want to locate potential friends among your online connections. By bridging online interactions with offline meetups, you keep relationships grounded in actual shared experiences.

Another consideration involves digital etiquette. Online arguments can escalate quickly due to the lack of tone, facial cues, and immediate feedback. If a friend's post offends you, approach the matter in a private message or phone call rather than engaging in a public debate. Similarly, be mindful when posting about shared experiences. If you have a habit of tagging friends in photos or sharing personal anecdotes, check they are comfortable with that. Overstepping these boundaries can create tension in your real-world friendship.

You should also watch out for time spent mindlessly scrolling. Social media can devour hours you might otherwise spend in direct conversations or face-to-face activities. If you catch yourself losing valuable time online, set limits. Turn those moments into real connections instead. A quick phone call, a text, or planning an outing with a friend might be far more fulfilling than browsing infinite feeds. By staying aware of how much time you invest on social platforms, you guard against letting virtual connections overshadow real bonds.

In short, social media is a tool. It can keep you linked across distances, but also encourage superficial contact if not used mindfully. Balanced usage, focusing on meaningful engagement and turning online acquaintances into real-life gatherings, lets you harness its benefits without undermining the depth your friendships need. By staying conscious of what you share, respecting privacy, and complementing virtual interactions with genuine communication, you ensure that your online friendships strengthen rather than replace authentic connection.

Overcoming Betrayal and Disappointment in Friendships

Trust can be broken in the closest friendships, often without warning. One day, you learn a friend has spoken behind your back, chosen not to stand by you during a crisis, or betrayed a confidence. The pain is real and can overshadow years of good memories, leaving you torn between disappointment and the longing to reclaim that bond. Though betrayal cuts deep, it does not automatically spell the end of the friendship. There may be a road to reconciliation, or you might decide it is time to move on.

Begin by allowing yourself to process the shock. You may feel anger, sadness, or confusion. Bottling these emotions can fuel bitterness, so let them surface in a constructive manner. Talk it over with a trusted confidant or write out your feelings in a private journal. Aim for clarity: what exactly hurt you, and why does it feel so personal? Sometimes betrayal hits not because of the act alone, but because it clashes starkly with the trust or loyalty you believed existed.

Once you are calmer, decide whether you want to address the issue with your friend. If you do, approach them in a straightforward, non-accusatory tone. Describe what you know or suspect, and explain how it affected you emotionally. Let them respond, as they may offer context or an apology. Genuine remorse and a willingness to make amends can signal a chance for healing. However, if they deny wrongdoing or turn the blame on you, it might confirm that the relationship lacks the honesty needed to mend.

Forgiveness can play a part, but it does not necessarily mean resuming the same level of closeness. If your friend's act was severe, you might forgive to release your anger yet still choose limited contact. For instance, you could restore polite acquaintance without confiding in them the way you used to. Alternatively, if their remorse is sincere and you sense the betrayal was situational, you may attempt full reconciliation. In that case, define new ground rules or boundaries. Both parties must commit to transparency, open discussion of grievances, and respect for each other's comfort levels.

It is natural to question your own judgment: "How did I not see this coming?" or "Should I have noticed red flags?" While introspection can help you grow, avoid self-blame. Friendships, like all human relationships, involve risk. That you trusted them in the first place means you were open and caring. A betrayal says more about their behaviour than your capacity to choose friends.

If you decide the friendship should end, allow yourself closure. This might involve an honest final conversation or a personal decision to stop contact gradually. Ending a friendship is never easy, especially if it once meant a lot. You may cycle through regret, nostalgia, or anger. Over time, that emotional storm will calm, particularly if you practice self-care. Lean on supportive friends, engage in uplifting activities, or try counselling if the hurt lingers deeply. Recognise this as a transformative chapter, teaching you to guard your trust more wisely, but without closing off your heart entirely.

Ultimately, betrayal can act as a harsh lesson in resilience. If addressed compassionately and fairly, some friendships emerge stronger, refined by shared acknowledgement of mistakes. Others end, paving the way for new connections that better align with your well-being. Whatever path you choose, your capacity to process, forgive, or move on affirms your determination to grow from even the most painful chapters in your friendship story.

How to Deepen Your Friendships

Deep friendship does not happen by chance. It calls for an intentional choice to invest time, effort, and vulnerability. If you find your bonds remain polite yet shallow, or you wish to transform an existing connection into something richer, you can take specific steps to encourage that closeness. True emotional intimacy with friends can provide a resilient support system and a source of mutual encouragement throughout life's phases.

Start with open conversations. Move away from routine small talk and ask meaningful questions. For instance, rather than only inquiring, "How's work?" you might say, "What has challenged you lately, and how are you feeling about it?" or "Any personal goals you are excited about?" At first, they might be surprised, especially if your chats were previously light. But once they sense you genuinely care, they may open up, providing a window into their inner world. Sharing about their challenges or hopes establishes a level of honesty that fosters deeper unity.

Active listening forms the next layer. You may find it tempting to interrupt with your experiences or solutions. Instead, slow down. Let them fully express themselves. Show you are present by maintaining comfortable eye contact or, if you are on a call, staying focused on their words rather than multitasking. Offer brief reflections like, "That sounds significant," or "I can see how that would affect you." This approach of listening with genuine empathy can transform an ordinary conversation into a powerful bonding experience.

Consider shared adventures beyond ordinary hangouts. If your friend loves nature, plan a weekend walk or a short getaway. If they are into cultural events, attend a local exhibition together. You might want to organise a creative activity, such as painting or cooking new dishes together. Joint experiences help you discover shared interests or hidden talents. Moreover, going through challenges or unfamiliar situations side by side can draw you closer. You recall these experiences fondly and continue building an emotional catalogue of shared memories.

Another tactic is vulnerability by example. If you are wishing for deeper friendship, you can lead by revealing a personal aspect of yourself. For instance, open up about a time you felt lonely or uncertain about your path. Your willingness to trust your friend with something meaningful is an invitation for them to trust you likewise. Vulnerability does not have to be grand revelations from the start, but it should reflect sincerity. Perhaps discuss a small worry or a recent disappointment. Over time, the cumulative effect of mutual sharing weaves a foundation of trust and compassion.

Lastly, remember that deepening a friendship is an ongoing practice. Follow up on details your friend has shared. If they mentioned a job interview, ask how it went. If they told you about a family issue, inquire about any updates. Such follow-through proves you are not only a passive listener but genuinely invested. This habit of consistent care can transform your relationship from acquaintances to confidants. Over time, these incremental actions build a solid sense of security and closeness, bridging the gap between an ordinary friend and a cherished companion you can rely on in every season of life.

Creating a Circle of Trust: Choosing Friends Wisely

Forming a close circle of friends is about intentionally choosing trustworthy individuals with whom you share values and mutual respect. While you may build many acquaintances, your inner circle should be carefully selected. These are the people who stand by you, speak truth in a caring manner, and respect your boundaries. By mindfully choosing who belongs in your most cherished circle, you invest in relationships that can last for years.

Examine the character of potential close friends. Look for signs of integrity, empathy, and reliability. Do they keep confidential information private, or do they casually gossip about mutual acquaintances? Someone who frequently reveals other people's personal matters may do the same with yours. Similarly, consistency in small promises can signal their reliability. If they consistently show up late or let you down, you might pause before elevating them into your tight-knit group.

Alignment of values plays a role. This does not mean you must agree on every topic, but fundamental principles like honesty and kindness help avoid tensions that breed distrust. If you are passionate about personal growth or spiritual reflection, having companions who encourage that side of you is crucial. You should sense that you do not have to defend your core beliefs. This harmony fosters a sense of ease, so your friendship is a source of support rather than conflict.

Watch how they respond when you are vulnerable. If they dismiss your emotions or respond with jokes, they may not be suited for your closest circle. Conversely, a friend who acknowledges your struggles and offers understanding is showing qualities that nurture trust. Over time, you see that such individuals create a safe space, making you comfortable to share your real challenges and joys.

Also, consider how you behave with them. A circle of trust is reciprocal. You strive to match the honesty and empathy you seek. If you appreciate a friend's openness, reflect that same level of sincerity back. When they confide in you, handle their words respectfully. Sustaining trust depends on both parties upholding these unwritten rules: you do not gossip about them, you keep your promises, and you stand by them if they face adversity.

Be ready to let go of potential toxicity. If you detect patterns of manipulation, envy, or harmful behaviour, it might be wise to keep that person at a distance. Sometimes, you discover that you get along in light-hearted contexts, yet they bring negativity or drama. It can be tough to reduce closeness with someone you have known for years, but your emotional well-being deserves protection. This is not about coldly discarding them but calmly placing them in a more peripheral slot among your friendships.

Ultimately, a well-chosen circle of trust offers mutual refuge. You share dreams and fears without fear of betrayal. These friends challenge you to become better, celebrate your achievements, and push you to face problems with courage. In return, you do the same for them. Though you may keep many loose connections, this smaller group becomes your emotional home, a place where acceptance and loyalty run deep. Taking the time to cultivate these bonds ensures you always have an anchor of support no matter what life brings.

The Joy of Rekindling Old Friendships

Reconnecting with an old friend can feel like stepping into a familiar room after a long absence. Memories resurface, stories flow, and you are reminded of who you once were. There is a comforting sense of continuity in picking up conversations that might have paused for months or even years. If done thoughtfully, rekindling such ties can add a rich layer to your current life.

Begin by reaching out gently. A simple message or call can suffice: "I was thinking about the time we travelled together and decided I would love to catch up. How have you been?" Keep your tone open and nostalgic, signalling that you remember shared experiences fondly. You might worry about whether they still care to hear from you, but in many cases, people appreciate the thought. They might have hesitated to contact you for the same reasons. An initial step on your part can dissolve the barriers of time and uncertainty.

In your first reconnected chat, avoid bombarding them with every detail of your life since you last spoke. Listen as well, focusing on understanding their current reality. They may have changed significantly. Perhaps they have new career paths, families, or passions that did not exist back then. Show genuine curiosity about these changes. Ask them to share what they are proud of, what challenges they have faced, or what dreams they are pursuing now.

Once you have both updated each other, reflect on shared memories. Mentioning past adventures can spark laughter and a sense of comfort, reminding you of what originally bonded you. This does not mean dwelling in the past entirely, but weaving old and new experiences together. If the friendship feels as if it has never left, you may pick up old jokes or references. That blend of nostalgia and current context can deepen the reconnection quickly.

However, be mindful of whether they still match your life values or remain an uplifting influence. It is possible that a friend from your younger years now embraces attitudes or lifestyles you find incompatible with your present self. If you sense toxicity or a fundamental clash, proceed with caution. You can still enjoy a polite conversation or occasional updates without forcing a tight bond. You have the power to decide how close you wish to get, based on your emotional health.

Another tip is to establish a new routine if the revived friendship seems promising. Suggest meeting monthly for a coffee, scheduling a video call, or engaging in an activity you both enjoy. Regular contact helps the friendship adapt to your current life, preventing it from drifting away yet again. Over time, these new interactions create fresh memories. That is how an old friend transitions into a current confidant, one who appreciates your history while growing alongside your present reality.

Rekindling old ties can be a beautiful experience. It offers a sense of continuity, bridging who you used to be with who you are now. You recall how you overcame past milestones, and you celebrate the progress both of you have achieved. These revived friendships also bring a perspective that no brand-new friend can offer, making them a valued treasure in your overall circle. Proceed with warmth, honesty, and openness, and see if the spark you once enjoyed can light a fresh chapter in both your lives.

Friendships Across Cultures: Learning and Growing Together

Friendships that span different cultures can broaden your worldview, enabling you to experience a new array of perspectives and traditions. In an increasingly interconnected world, you may frequently encounter individuals from various backgrounds, whether through work, travelling, or academic pursuits. Approaching these opportunities with curiosity and empathy paves the way for deep bonds that transcend borders.

One of the most immediate ways to bridge cultural gaps is active listening. Let your friend describe their upbringing, traditions, or beliefs. They might recount holidays unique to their country, the foods they grew up eating, or the nuances of their language. Show interest with thoughtful questions, not for polite small talk but to truly grasp the deeper meaning behind their words. Such engagement reaffirms that you value their identity. In turn, they may feel inspired to learn about your background. This mutual exchange fosters a space of shared respect and exploration.

Language differences can pose hurdles, but they also present ways to bond. Sometimes, you will communicate in a common language, though not your mother tongue, leading to humorous mistakes or moments of clarity. Laughing together about small misunderstandings can strengthen your rapport. If you pick up basic greetings or phrases from their language, it often delights them and shows genuine willingness to connect. They might reciprocate by learning expressions from you, creating a playful atmosphere of mutual learning.

Cultural friendships also challenge stereotypes. Perhaps you held assumptions about certain practices or attitudes based on limited media portrayals. Directly hearing a friend's account often dismantles those preconceptions. You discover that their daily life is more layered than you assumed, shaped by personal history rather than simple cultural labels. This broadening of horizons does not only reflect the friend's culture but encourages you to question your own biases. You become more open to variety in human experiences.

Shared experiences can reinforce cultural friendships. Invite them to accompany you to local events or gatherings. Let them see your favourite hangouts, taste your home cooking, or meet family members. Conversely, visit their cultural festivals, sample their cuisine, and attend ceremonies important to them. These immersive activities bring your experiences to life, bridging any knowledge gaps. You also gain a sense of how your ways are perceived from a fresh viewpoint, inspiring you to reassess or appreciate familiar norms.

Consider the complexities of tradition. You might disagree with certain customs or beliefs. If that arises, aim for calm discussions. You might say, "I find it challenging to understand this aspect of your tradition; would you explain more?" Instead of casting judgement, ask for context. They might share the historical or spiritual reasons behind a practice. While you might not fully adopt their viewpoint, you build empathy. These civil conversations can draw you closer, showing that you can hold differing opinions while maintaining respect.

Over time, cross-cultural friendships can become some of the most rewarding. They encourage you to adopt new tastes, question unexamined habits, and discover fresh ways of thinking. Such ties are not without effort, but the payoff is considerable: you gain a friend who connects you to a broader human story, and they gain the same in you. Your identity expands through the meeting of differences, proving that authenticity and kindness can unify people from every corner of the globe.

Letting Go with Love: When Friendships Naturally End

While you work hard to maintain meaningful friendships, there are times when a bond has run its course. Perhaps you and a friend drift apart due to shifting values, physical distance, or fundamental changes in personality. Alternatively, unresolved conflict or repeated disappointments might drive a wedge that cannot be mended. In these circumstances, choosing to end or lessen the connection can be the compassionate option, sparing both of you further resentment or emotional strain.

Recognising the signs is the first step. You might notice that every interaction feels forced or tense, leaving you more drained than energised. Conversations revolve around the past rather than shared hopes. Arguments flare easily, or silence fills the gaps. If these patterns persist despite attempts at open dialogue, it might indicate that the friendship no longer offers the mutual understanding it once did. Rather than labelling it a failure, you can accept that your journeys have diverged.

Choosing to let go with love means parting ways respectfully. If you opt to discuss it openly, focus on how you feel rather than launching accusations. "I cherish the times we had, but lately, I sense we have grown in different directions," or "I think we are struggling to connect the way we used to, and it may be healthier for both of us to step back." This honest approach can be emotional, but it minimises bitterness by emphasising that you still hold regard for the bond you once shared.

Sometimes, a friend might not see the situation in the same way. They may want to salvage it, pushing for more conversations or changes. You can attempt mediation or structured talks if you believe there is potential. However, if repeated efforts do not resolve underlying issues, letting go might remain the wisest path. By being firm yet empathetic, you reduce the likelihood of a messy fallout.

It is also possible that there is no final sit-down chat, particularly if the drifting happened naturally over a long period. In that scenario, you might quietly accept the distance. You no longer initiate calls or meet-ups, and your friend seems to reciprocate by not reaching out. Although this approach can feel unsaid, it sometimes reflects a mutual understanding that your paths have separated. If you find peace in that quiet departure, it could be the gentlest closure. You can still hold them in fond memory, acknowledging the role they played in shaping you up to this point.

Letting go can prompt a sense of grief, as you might mourn the lost closeness or memories built over years. Give yourself space to feel sadness or reflect on the lessons learned. This process can also highlight how you have grown.

Friendship: The Bonds That Sustain Us

You recognise that relationships, much like life stages, do not remain static. By releasing connections that no longer serve you or the other person, you free each other to form new bonds aligned with your evolving selves.

Letting go with love also means no negative campaigning against the person. You do not disparage them to mutual friends or air grudges publicly. Instead, you carry a quiet respect for what once was, grateful for the experiences shared. Over time, you can look back without malice, seeing the friendship as a chapter of your life that contributed to the person you are today. That gentle closure paves the way for new friendships to flourish, each marking a fresh beginning in your unfolding story.

In Conclusion

You have now explored the essence of friendships in adulthood, discovering how they grow, adapt, and sometimes fade away. By nurturing qualities like trust, empathy, and open communication, you transform acquaintances into long-lasting allies. Technology, life changes, and occasional betrayals test these bonds, but with honest dialogue and mutual respect, you can navigate such hurdles successfully.

Next, you will shift your focus to different forms of relationships, such as romantic bonds or professional connections, reinforcing the underlying principle that all interactions flourish when grounded in understanding and shared purpose. Carry forward the insights gained about genuine communication and mutual support, and you will find you are well-prepared for the chapters to come.

Chapter 7

Romantic Connections: Aligning Souls

Romantic relationships tap into your deepest emotions, reflecting both your aspirations and unresolved fears. These bonds go beyond simple companionship. They mirror your growth, reveal your vulnerabilities, and can propel you toward new insights. Love in its various forms invites you to share your innermost dreams and sorrows with another, forging an emotional union that transcends casual interaction.

This chapter navigates the many layers of romantic connections. You will explore how energy dynamics influence your bond, how communication acts as its lifeblood, and how you sustain individuality even within a shared life. Whether you are aiming to keep your existing relationship thriving or are open to encountering a soulmate or twin flame, these pages offer perspective on aligning your souls. By the end, you will see that romance involves two individuals, each on their path, yet uniting to create something that is both supportive and transformative.

The Energy Dynamics of Love Relationships

Romantic bonds are alive with energy, an invisible current that shapes how you and your partner respond to each other. At the outset of a relationship, you might feel an electric pull, where your shared excitement generates a sense of warmth. The way this energy flows between you determines whether

Romantic Connections: Aligning Souls

your connection remains harmonious or becomes fraught with tension.

You can spot energy dynamics in simple day-to-day moments. If you sense your partner's stress from a taxing workday, you might pick up on their agitated tone. In reaction, you become uneasy, possibly snapping back, and the emotional current spirals. On the other hand, if you manage to stay calm and understanding, you may shift the atmosphere, offering reassurance that dissolves their anxiety. This interplay demonstrates how your energy states, positive or negative, meld and influence each other.

The Law of Attraction mindset teaches that your inner vibration can attract or repel experiences. In romantic terms, if your heart brims with self-love and kindness, you are more likely to connect with someone who shares those qualities. Conversely, unresolved anger or self-doubt might draw in similar negativity. This is not about blaming yourself if a relationship goes wrong, but about appreciating the power your emotional state holds in shaping your love life.

Maintaining a balanced energy within the relationship means being aware of how you handle your own emotional states. Do you regularly vent your frustrations without seeking to resolve them? Or do you endeavour to calm yourself before talking through conflicts? If you pour negativity into every argument, it triggers your partner's defences, perpetuating a cycle of stress. However, if you approach discussions with mindfulness and empathy, the relationship's overall energy becomes one of collaboration rather than combat.

Another aspect is recognising when external influences disrupt your relationship's flow. Long work hours, unresolved family drama, or financial tension can tarnish your personal energy and seep into romantic exchanges. Checking in with each other to identify sources of stress creates an environment of empathy. By naming these stressors, "I am feeling strained by finances" or "I have unresolved issues with my parent", you prevent confusion that arises when one partner's mood shifts abruptly without explanation.

You should also remember that energy in love relationships is not solely about avoiding negativity. High vibrations of joy, affection, and enthusiasm can elevate the bond. A playful spirit and readiness to celebrate small achievements bring lightness into daily interactions. Compliments, heartfelt thank-yous, and spontaneous signs of affection foster a cycle of positive resonance. Couples who swap daily affirmations or indulge in shared humour often discover a deep sense of connection that makes them more resilient when problems arise.

Hence, the energy dynamic in a relationship is fluid. It changes daily, influenced by external demands, personal well-being, and the emotional climate you co-create. Observing and actively steering this energy, both individually and together, safeguards your bond from becoming drained by stress or negativity. By treating the relationship as a living entity needing consistent nurturing, you anchor it in supportive energy, setting the stage for a romance that encourages both partners to flourish.

Recognising a Soul Mate or Twin Flame

You might have heard stories of soul mates, relationships that feel destined, or twin flames, said to be a mirror of your own soul. Recognising such a bond can be exhilarating yet perplexing. You experience an immediate familiarity that transcends normal attraction. Conversations flow naturally, as though you have always known each other, even if you met recently. The question is how to distinguish a profound connection from a passing infatuation.

A soul mate connection, broadly defined, is a relationship where both parties complement each other's growth while sharing a strong emotional bond. It may be comfortable, supportive, and a source of safety for both of you. A sense of synchronicity appears in how your paths align, or how you repeatedly cross each other's orbit until you finally meet. Though you remain separate individuals, the emotional synergy feels like a snug fit. You feel seen, heard, and understood in ways you might rarely experience with others.

A twin flame, on the other hand, is often depicted as a more intense version of that synergy, sometimes featuring profound highs and lows. The legend suggests that twin flames challenge you to face deeper insecurities, prompting radical self-discovery. While exhilarating, these relationships can be tumultuous if neither is ready to handle the intense reflection they impose. Rather than being purely romantic bliss, twin flames can force you to confront emotional baggage, making them both transformative and potentially stormy.

One sign is the sense of "instant recognition." It might be an inexplicable pull that suggests, "I feel like I already know you," or a deep resonance with how they speak and think. This bond might not always appear as a lightning bolt of passion; it can also grow more subtly as repeated encounters reveal a level of mutual resonance. Often, you feel comfortable dropping your guard early on, discussing personal convictions or hidden aspirations that you might usually keep private until much later.

A hallmark of these connections is mutual transformation. A soul mate or twin flame does not merely revolve around romantic euphoria. Rather, they inspire your personal growth, perhaps challenging you to break free of old limitations. In turn, you contribute to their evolution. This reciprocal development extends beyond typical romance, weaving spiritual or philosophical dimensions into your bond. You might notice you pick up new hobbies, refine your worldview, or heal past wounds through your interactions with them.

Yet be cautious of romanticising these concepts. A strong initial spark does not guarantee a healthy or lasting partnership. Soul mate or twin flame relationships still require mutual respect, communication, and compromise. If someone uses the idea of being your twin flame to rationalise poor treatment or manipulation, that is a red flag. Regardless of the spiritual label, a truly fulfilling connection is anchored by kindness and responsibility.

In summary, a soul mate or twin flame bond might appear as a deeply intuitive affinity, a sense of destined convergence, or a mirror that exposes your deepest challenges and gifts. Whether calm and steady or fiery and intense, these relationships serve as catalysts for growth. While the magic of initial recognition might dazzle you, it is the consistent effort and shared aspiration that sustain any profound love. By nurturing open communication, empathy, and honesty, you give such a special bond the grounding it needs to evolve into something lasting.

Romantic Connections: Aligning Souls

Communication: The Heartbeat of Romance

When you think about a thriving romance, your mind may conjure images of affectionate gestures or shared getaways. Yet behind these scenes, effective communication remains the key that binds you together. You can be deeply in love, yet if you fail to articulate your desires, concerns, or appreciation, misunderstandings inevitably arise. Good communication breathes life into relationships, serving as the foundation on which intimacy and emotional safety are built.

One of the simplest steps is learning to speak from personal feelings rather than flinging blame. If something troubles you, phrase your concerns as, "I feel hurt when..." instead of, "You always do this..." By focusing on how you experience an action, you reduce the chance your partner will feel attacked. This approach fosters empathy. They listen to your feelings rather than defending themselves from an accusation.

Equally important is the art of listening. Hearing your partner means more than letting them speak until you can retort. Practice active listening by reflecting on what they say. For instance, if they mention feeling lonely, you might reply, "It sounds like you have been feeling overlooked," verifying that you have understood them. That small act of paraphrasing shows genuine interest, making them feel valued. It also clarifies any vague or ambiguous statements.

Nonverbal cues form part of relationship communication. Pay attention to body language, facial expressions, and tone. A partner might say they are fine, but their posture or voice reveals otherwise. If you sense tension, gently open a path for dialogue: "I notice you seem quieter than usual. Are you bothered by something?" This direct, caring approach can prevent simmering resentments from escalating.

Timing and environment matter. Avoid raising major issues at stressful moments, such as when your partner arrives home exhausted or while rushing to meet a deadline. Seek a calm interval, free from distractions, where both can focus. Turning off phones or stepping away from daily noise sets a respectful stage. That deliberate choice to invest time and attention signals, "Your viewpoint matters."

Honesty is crucial, although it must be handled with sensitivity. There is a difference between bluntness that wounds and honest sincerity that aims to build mutual understanding. If you have reservations about a sensitive topic, explain why. "I am nervous to mention this, but I need to be truthful." This admission of vulnerability often inspires empathy. It underscores that you trust your partner enough to share your raw emotions without fear of scorn.

Lastly, keep the conversation balanced. If you find yourself doing most of the talking, step back and invite your partner's input. If your partner frequently dominates, voice that you would like to share your thoughts as well. Establishing a mutual exchange ensures both perspectives are heard, preventing hidden resentments. Through consistent practice of open dialogue and attentive listening, your romance grows resilient. Instead of letting unspoken hurts fester, you deal with them as a team, forging a deeper sense of companionship. In this way, communication stands as the heartbeat of your love story, pumping vitality and connection into every corner of your shared life.

Maintaining Individuality Within a Union

Romantic Connections: Aligning Souls

Romantic relationships thrive when you unite in love yet keep a sense of your distinct identity. It is easy to become consumed by the partnership, focusing on joint goals and time spent together, but losing your personal interests or friendships can create an imbalance. Over time, sacrificing individuality may lead to resentment or a stifling sense of having nowhere to breathe freely. A healthy union balances closeness with autonomy.

One of the first indicators of diminishing individuality is when personal hobbies fall by the wayside. You stop painting or forget weekly meetups with friends because you would rather spend every moment with your partner. While it seems romantic initially, in the long term, you might realise you miss those outlets that nourished your creativity or sense of self. Retaining your own passions not only supports your well-being but also keeps you intriguing. When you return from an afternoon enjoying your craft or a workout session, you bring fresh energy back into the relationship.

Separate social circles can also enrich your bond. Maybe your partner loves mountain climbing with a close friend, while you attend a local reading group. Having these separate spheres of interaction fosters a sense of independence, allowing each of you to bring new stories and perspectives home. You both appreciate that space is not a sign of disinterest; it is a chance to enjoy growth individually. Then, when you reconvene, you share your experiences with renewed enthusiasm.

Boundaries shape how you maintain individuality. If your partner attempts to micromanage your free time, you may feel smothered. Gently clarify your need for personal space, whether that is a quiet hour for reflection or an evening with your friends. By asserting these lines kindly yet firmly, you let them know that you love them while caring for your own needs. Ideally, they follow suit, ensuring both parties respect each other's autonomy.

Communication plays a part here. Reassure your partner that you are not pulling away emotionally by pursuing your own goals. Emphasise that your bond grows stronger when both of you are content. If they worry about losing you, invite them to discuss these fears. Perhaps you can find a middle ground: you keep your solo time, but also arrange regular shared moments so no one feels neglected.

Another aspect is preserving personal dreams within the partnership. While you might have joint ambitions, like purchasing a home or travelling together, you also have personal milestones. If you want to acquire a specialised skill or train for a sports event, do not abandon those aims for the sake of the relationship. Instead, share these aspirations, seeking your partner's support. Encouraging each other's independent goals creates mutual respect. Each of you flourishes, and the relationship becomes a place of shared pride rather than competition or restriction.

Maintaining individuality is not about secrecy or pulling away. It is about honouring what makes you unique while embracing the union you have chosen. That space to be yourself, to chase personal interests, and to keep supportive friendships ensures your well of self-worth remains abundant. You do not lose who you are by loving someone deeply. Rather, you let your distinct selves shine, adding variety and vibrancy to the relationship, so both you and your partner feel fulfilled, connected, and free.

The Role of Intimacy and Vulnerability

Intimacy in romantic relationships goes well beyond physical closeness; it involves emotional and sometimes spiritual dimensions as well. Being truly intimate means opening your inner world, your fears, hopes, and fondest memories, to your partner. This transparency requires a bold step: vulnerability. You may find it challenging to reveal uncertain parts of yourself for fear of being judged or hurt, yet that same openness can lead to the most profound connection you will ever share.

Emotional intimacy starts with small but meaningful exposures of your inner thoughts. Instead of glossing over your day with "I am fine," let your partner in on your genuine emotional landscape. Maybe you felt uneasy during a meeting or disappointed by a friend's comments. Verbalising these feelings deepens trust. In response, your partner might share their own hidden concerns, resulting in a space where neither of you feels the need to put on a façade.

Physical intimacy also relies on vulnerability. Letting another person see your unguarded physical and emotional self can be unnerving. If, for example, you have insecurities about your body, gently discussing them can ease tension, reminding you that love does not demand perfection. With kind communication, you learn to see closeness not as a performance but as a mutual discovery. As confidence grows, you may find physical connection becomes more fulfilling, reflecting the sincerity of your shared emotional ground.

Overcoming fear of judgement is central to vulnerability. You might worry, "What if they think I am too sensitive or clingy?" or "What if they do not handle my secret gracefully?" While caution is normal, trust-building is impossible without risking some level of disclosure. Approach these moments gradually. Perhaps begin with something small: mention a personal disappointment or a dream you rarely discuss. If your partner responds with empathy, try deeper revelations next time.

Boundaries and communication provide guidance on what to share, when to share it, and how to handle each other's confessions. For instance, if a memory from your past triggers intense emotions, let your partner know that you are opening a vulnerable part of yourself and would appreciate gentle understanding. This heads-up helps them offer the caring response you need. If they slip up or tease you unknowingly, correct them kindly. Emphasise, "That comment hurts because it makes me feel ridiculed at a sensitive moment." Over time, you teach each other the right approach to handling emotional rawness.

It is important to note that vulnerability is a two-way street. If you consistently share personal aspects of your life but your partner remains aloof, you might feel unbalanced. In such situations, encourage them to voice their inner thoughts, reminding them that you are not there to criticise. Suggest simple steps, like discussing the highlight of their day or a small worry they have been carrying. This approach fosters mutual revelation, which is crucial for real intimacy.

When vulnerability thrives in a relationship, intimacy becomes a living current that draws you closer. You handle disagreements with deeper compassion, acknowledging the sensitive triggers that lie beneath surface arguments. Physical closeness feels more authentic, rooted in emotional safety. The result is a bond that endures because it is built on genuine sharing, not the masks you wear to appear strong or unflawed. By embracing vulnerability, you discover love's power to bind two individuals in a shared emotional realm far richer than either could know alone.

Overcoming Challenges Together: Strengthening Your Bond

No matter how well you mesh, every couple faces tough moments, whether from external pressures or disagreements that erupt from differing viewpoints. It is in these challenging times that your bond is truly tested. The key is embracing a mindset of collaboration rather than confrontation. When you treat challenges as shared hurdles, you shift the dynamic from "You versus Me" to "Us versus the problem."

One way to approach adversity together is to create a safe space for problem-solving. For instance, schedule a dedicated time for discussing a recurring issue. Sit down without distractions such as phones or television. Start by outlining the problem in neutral terms: "We have been struggling to balance household chores," rather than flinging accusations like "You never do your part." Presenting the problem objectively sets a constructive tone. Each partner can then offer ideas, and you weigh the merits of each together. This approach fosters unity, showing you are equally invested in finding a resolution.

When emotions flare during these discussions, pause if needed. The phrase "Let us take a break and come back to this" might save you from saying regretful words. De-escalating tension early prevents small disagreements from escalating into major disputes that harm the relationship. Sometimes, a short walk or a few deep breaths is enough to regain composure and continue productively. This tactic emphasises that your relationship matters more than winning an argument.

Accepting personal responsibility also promotes teamwork. Even if your partner triggered your frustration, you can reflect on your own reactions. Could you have responded more calmly? Owning your part of the conflict means you are less likely to see yourself as purely a victim. In tandem, invite your partner to examine their own behaviour. With both parties acknowledging their role in misunderstandings, the bond strengthens because you each see that you are responsible for the environment you create.

In some cases, external help is beneficial. If you repeatedly clash over finances, for example, consult a financial adviser or counsellor who can offer a neutral perspective. If the challenge relates to communication breakdown, couples therapy might help identify unspoken patterns. Seeking outside support is not a weakness but a sign that you value your connection enough to gather resources that facilitate healthier interaction.

After you work through a significant challenge, celebrate the progress. Perhaps you overcame a stressful period of unemployment, navigated an illness, or resolved a conflict about future goals. Acknowledge that you surmounted this hurdle as a team. Sharing gratitude for each other's patience and adaptability reminds you why you are stronger as a unit. This sense of shared victory fosters resilience. When fresh trials appear, you can recall how you previously overcame adversities together, trusting that your combined efforts will see you through again.

Ultimately, challenges are catalysts for growth. While no one likes disagreements or external setbacks, they can push you to communicate better, refine priorities, and deepen empathy. The approach you adopt, focusing on partnership rather than blame, makes the difference. Each adversity becomes an opportunity to fortify trust, proving to both of you that this love stands firm, not only in sunny moments but in the heart of life's storms.

Healing Together: Working Through Past Traumas

Many individuals carry emotional wounds from childhood or past relationships, and these can resurface in romance. You may notice triggers that spark fear, anger, or withdrawal, puzzling your partner if they do not know the root causes. Healing in a relationship context involves recognising each other's backstories, offering patience, and acting as supportive allies during emotional flashbacks or anxiety.

One important step is open disclosure of any significant trauma you bring. Although it can feel daunting, confiding in your partner about painful episodes, such as childhood neglect or past betrayal, reduces misinterpretation of your reactions. Instead of seeing your guarded responses as coldness, they understand them as protective measures shaped by old scars. This clarity often increases their compassion and encourages them to adapt their behaviour to help you feel secure.

In turn, be receptive if your partner shares their own vulnerabilities. People cope with trauma differently. Some prefer quiet reflection; others find comfort in talking through details. Let them direct how much they want to reveal at once. Refrain from pushing them to detail every aspect if they are not ready. Affirm your willingness to listen and remain patient. This approach signals your respect for their healing pace.

Professional help can enhance this joint healing. Couples therapy with a trauma-informed counsellor provides guidance on managing triggers and building coping strategies. Therapists may teach you both how to communicate during flashbacks or offer techniques for defusing stress when old memories threaten to derail a calm conversation. The aim is not to re-traumatise either party but to integrate past pain more healthily. By practising these methods, your partnership grows into a sanctuary of mutual understanding.

It also helps to create consistent routines that reinforce safety. Perhaps you establish a ritual of hugging for a few minutes each morning or regularly check in with each other in the evening, asking about emotional well-being. Such rituals can counteract the unpredictability experienced in traumatic histories. Your partner realises they have a stable, reliable anchor in you, and you trust the relationship's steadiness to handle emotional waves. Over time, these small acts of consistency help to reprogram your sense of what a safe connection looks like.

Boundaries remain vital. Supporting your partner's healing does not mean becoming their perpetual therapist. Ensure self-care so you do not burn out emotionally. If your partner's trauma leads to anger or destructive behaviour toward you, that is unacceptable. You can stand by them while urging professional help, but also maintain your own boundaries. Love is powerful, but it must not blind you to the need for mutual respect.

Healing together can strengthen your relationship profoundly. By bravely confronting buried pain, you and your partner bond through empathy. You witness each other's raw states and learn to provide comfort without judgment. These experiences carve out a deep intimacy that can overshadow fleeting conflicts. Instead of separate journeys, you walk side by side, acknowledging each other's past but building a future free from its grip. Through honesty, structured support, and unwavering understanding, your shared love becomes both the backdrop and the engine of genuine healing.

The Importance of Shared Goals and Dreams

Romantic relationships flourish when you both share a sense of direction, uniting around common aims. While individuality matters, having overlapping dreams or plans can create a powerful bond. You sense you are not only companions in the present but also co-authors of a shared future. Whether the goal is building a family, travelling the world, or launching a business, working toward it together deepens your sense of purpose.

A crucial first step is finding alignment. This does not mean agreeing on everything. However, if one of you is determined to travel long-term while the other is devoted to staying rooted in one spot, tension arises. Talk about personal ambitions early on. "What do you imagine for your life in five or ten years?" or "Is raising children essential to you?" By exchanging views, you discover areas of harmony or potential friction. When you know each other's core objectives, you can either adapt or discuss compromise strategies.

Shared goals also provide motivation. When you see your partner working diligently toward a joint ambition, it can drive you to put forth your best effort. The synergy created by mutual dedication is uplifting, as every small achievement becomes something you celebrate together. Suppose you plan to buy a house, so both of you adopt budgeting measures. Each success, like paying off a loan or setting aside an emergency fund, is not solely an individual triumph but a step for your united journey.

However, it is vital to stay flexible. Dreams can shift as your perspectives evolve or external circumstances change. Perhaps you originally envisioned living abroad, but as the years pass, your career opportunities or personal priorities lead you to another path. Revisit your shared goals periodically. Ask each other, "Do we still want this? Has anything changed for us?" That ongoing dialogue ensures you do not drift apart, clinging to an outdated vision. Instead, you shape a fresh plan that suits who you both are now.

Supporting your partner's personal dreams can also be part of having shared goals. You might not share a specific aspiration, like training for a marathon or writing a novel, but you can back each other enthusiastically. That backing transforms their individual wish into a collective enterprise in spirit, if not in direct participation. You might help them find resources or provide moral support. When they succeed, the victory reverberates throughout your relationship, strengthening your bond.

Finally, remember that day-to-day living is more than chasing distant goals. Balance your long-range plans with enjoyment of the present moment. If you only focus on future milestones, you risk missing the small joys of your partnership right now. Arrange time to relax together, reflect on achievements so far, and express gratitude for each step. These shared affirmations reinforce unity, reminding you both that the ultimate aim is not purely about a destination. It is about growing side by side, celebrating progress along the path, and adapting as needed. With shared goals in place, you develop a sense of shared identity. Each challenge along the way becomes easier to handle because it is never a solo mission. You face life as allies, fuelling each other's determination to bring your joint vision to life.

Rekindling the Spark: Keeping Love Alive

Long-term relationships can slip into a comfortable routine that might lack the excitement of the initial months. Although stability is a cherished aspect of love, you do not want predictability to replace passion entirely. Keeping the spark alive is about injecting creativity and maintaining a sense of wonder toward each other, even after years spent side by side.

Surprises refresh your bond. A thoughtful note left on the table, an unexpected small gift of something they have casually mentioned wanting, or planning a local day out, all break up the monotony of everyday routines. These gestures do not have to be lavish. Their power lies in showing that you remain attentive. You notice your partner's unspoken wishes or changes in mood and respond in a way that reminds them you treasure them.

Spending quality time free from electronic distractions is equally helpful. Cooking a meal together without checking your phone or scheduling a long walk in nature fosters deeper conversations. During these uninterrupted moments, revisit favourite memories or discuss your aspirations. Nostalgia can revive old warmth, prompting you to recall why you fell in love. It also sets the stage to envision the future collectively, giving a renewed sense of direction.

Revisiting the early days can jolt you out of complacency. Plan a "date night" reminiscent of when you first met, choosing a restaurant you used to love or even wearing something that reminds you of your early courtship. This playful approach rekindles youthful excitement. Some couples enjoy flipping through old pictures or rereading the messages they exchanged while dating. These reminders can reignite affectionate feelings often dulled by stress or daily obligations.

Another strategy to reignite passion is to keep personal growth alive. If you expand your skills or knowledge, you introduce new dynamics to the relationship. Perhaps you take up a dance class or learn a musical instrument. As your partner sees you evolving, they discover fresh aspects of your personality. There is intrigue in recognising that you are not static. Likewise, encourage them to pursue their own interests. Each new achievement or interest is a conversation starter, preventing the relationship from turning stale.

Physical intimacy also benefits from deliberate attention. The initial novelty of physical connection may fade over time, but you can revitalise it by exploring new ways of closeness, whether that is a gentle back massage or a change of environment. Keeping honest conversations about comfort levels and trying small surprises fosters a sense of ongoing discovery. You do not need to attempt anything extreme. Even small changes, like lighting candles or creating a softer

Romantic Connections: Aligning Souls

ambience, can elevate the experience and break routine habits.

By proactively introducing excitement and depth, you remind each other that love can grow richer rather than fade. The spark is not solely about grand romantic gestures; it lies in consistent efforts to stay curious about your partner. Their personality and dreams do not freeze in time. If you remain eager to learn who they are becoming, the spark can evolve into a steady flame that keeps romance warm through all life's seasons.

When to Hold On and When to Let Go

Romance can be challenging, and you might wonder whether perseverance or release is the right path. Perhaps your relationship faces chronic problems, or you sense a persistent feeling that something is off. Recognising when to keep working on the bond and when to accept that it has run its course is no easy decision. Yet clarity here can save both you and your partner undue pain, ensuring you both find a way forward that respects your well-being.

First, assess the nature of the difficulties. If you face common obstacles, like communication lapses, differing schedules, or financial strains, these can often be fixed through mutual effort. You might try couples counselling, or you can create fresh routines, adjusting daily interactions to reduce friction. Such steps might reignite cooperation. The willingness to address issues head-on signals that neither partner is ready to abandon the relationship. The question is whether you both commit to improving it.

However, some issues run deeper, such as consistent disrespect or emotional neglect. If your partner belittles your aspirations or you feel unsafe speaking your mind, that is not a minor disagreement. A healthy relationship requires basic respect and emotional security. If attempts to rectify such issues repeatedly fail, it could indicate a fundamental mismatch. No matter how loyal or patient you are, you cannot salvage a bond that consistently violates your dignity.

Observe how your partner responds when you raise serious concerns. Do they brush them aside or become hostile, or do they show genuine regret and a plan for change? If the other party dismisses your distress or undermines your attempts at resolution, your energy may be best redirected toward an environment that nurtures you. On the other hand, if they listen earnestly and show tangible signs of adjusting, your patience may pay off.

Holding on also means gauging your emotional reserves. Are you fully drained, feeling anxious or depressed due to this union? You might endure a short phase of discomfort while you both adapt new habits, but if months or years pass without relief, you must reflect on whether the cost is too high. A relationship is not merely about soldiering on for its own sake. It should elevate your life's quality in some fundamental way.

It is equally vital to review whether you still share overarching goals or values. If your dream of having children conflicts with your partner's unwavering desire to remain child-free, love alone may not overcome that gap. In such irreversible differences, walking away might preserve your long-term happiness. Though heartbreak follows, it might free both of you to find more suitable matches.

When you do decide to let go, do so respectfully. Avoid heated confrontations or blame games. Share your reasons compassionately. If at all possible, part on terms that grant closure and mutual respect. That approach spares you additional emotional wounds and allows each side to heal over time, cherishing the positive experiences you did share.

Ultimately, deciding to hold on or let go is deeply personal. No external checklist can dictate it for you. However, by observing your emotional health, watching your partner's willingness to grow, and checking alignment in values, you can find a direction grounded in honesty. Whether you stay and rebuild or end the relationship with love, you honour the truth of what each of you needs from love and from life.

In Conclusion

In this chapter, you have examined the multifaceted nature of romantic connections, from spotting deep soul-level bonds to sustaining individuality within committed relationships. You have seen how healthy communication, mutual support, and shared dreams uplift love while letting vulnerability guide you to genuine intimacy. At times, you might confront challenges that demand teamwork or require you to choose whether to push forward or part ways. Through it all, the central theme stands: alignment of energy, empathy, and respect propels any romance toward deeper fulfilment.

Next, your perspective widens to your professional life, where relationships also flourish or wither. The upcoming chapter will show you how to foster positivity and collaboration in the workplace, forging strong professional connections rooted in emotional intelligence and respect. By applying your relationship skills beyond personal circles,

Connections

you will see how positivity and good communication elevate every area of life.

Chapter 8

The Workplace: Building Positive Professional Connections

Work occupies much of your daily schedule, so your office environment has a powerful influence on your mood and motivation. Fostering positive professional connections is more than a path to career success; it creates a harmonious space where you and your colleagues can collaborate effectively. This chapter presents strategies for improving relationships with your team, supervisor, and the wider organisation. By employing empathy, assertiveness, and a clear sense of boundaries, you can help establish a workplace that values growth, shared respect, and productivity.

These pages will explore diverse elements, from emotional intelligence and supportive culture to managing personality conflicts. You will learn to recognise and neutralise negative presences, often dubbed workplace "Energy Vampires", without losing your own spark. As you adapt these insights, you will not only advance your professional objectives but also preserve your well-being. This holistic approach demonstrates that success and empathy can go hand in hand, ensuring that your work life is not merely about tasks and deadlines but also about meaningful human interactions.

The Importance of Emotional Intelligence at Work

Connections

Workplaces can be stressful, often demanding time-bound achievements and dealing with varied personalities. In these fast-paced settings, you might emphasise expertise or efficiency, yet emotional intelligence often proves more critical to success and harmony. This quality involves understanding your own emotions, empathising with colleagues, and effectively navigating interpersonal exchanges. When you tap into emotional intelligence, you contribute to a balanced atmosphere where productivity and morale flourish side by side. The first key is self-awareness. At work, you might face tight deadlines or challenging projects that test your patience. If you are unaware of how stress or frustration is building up, you might snap at a colleague or come across as harsh in team chats. By regularly checking your emotional state, asking, "Am I feeling anxious, impatient, or overwhelmed?", you can make more conscious decisions about how you respond. Instead of letting tension dictate your reactions, you step away for a short break or calmly articulate your needs, such as requesting an extended timeline or dividing tasks differently.

Self-regulation is the next step. Recognising an emotion is crucial, but you also need to handle it responsibly. Perhaps you detect frustration creeping in when a colleague repeatedly interrupts. Rather than delivering a sharp retort, you practise a short pause. Take a steady breath, then respond with a measured statement like, "I would like to finish my point; can I continue?" This approach signals your respect for the environment and sets a professional tone.

Empathy transforms how you relate to colleagues or customers. For instance, if a junior teammate misses a deadline, you might feel annoyed. However, if you learn that

The Workplace: Building Positive Professional Connections

they are juggling multiple new responsibilities, your perspective softens. You might say, "I understand this is your first month handling these tasks. Let us figure out a plan to manage them more effectively." This empathy does not excuse negligence but shows willingness to help them improve. Such leadership fosters loyalty and openness within the team.

Social skills, another aspect of emotional intelligence, handle how you build rapport, negotiate conflict, and inspire collaboration. If you consistently check in with your peers on a personal level, "How are you managing your workload? Anything you need?" you create an environment that values each individual. When disagreements arise, you approach them with solution-oriented questions rather than pointing fingers. Over time, colleagues see you as approachable. They are more likely to ask for help or share concerns early, allowing the team to resolve issues before they escalate.

Additionally, motivation under emotional intelligence means drawing from internal drives rather than external pressures. A colleague who is intrinsically motivated to excel or learn fosters a positive influence around them. Others sense that genuine enthusiasm and become more eager to contribute. Workplaces can become cycles of high morale when leaders and teams combine clarity of purpose with an uplifting spirit.

By weaving self-awareness, self-regulation, empathy, social skills, and sound motivation into your professional approach, you cultivate an emotionally intelligent style that yields a supportive culture. This culture sees setbacks not as reasons to blame but as chances to grow. It also encourages employees to treat each other with respect and understanding, which, in turn, drives higher performance and overall job satisfaction. The result is a synergy in which everyone's best is brought out, demonstrating that emotional intelligence is not just a personal asset but a cornerstone of professional achievement.

Cultivating a Positive Work Environment

A positive work environment affects both team efficiency and individual satisfaction. When you walk into an office filled with respect, encouragement, and collaboration, daily tasks become easier to handle. Low stress levels and clear communication also boost creativity, leading to innovative solutions. Yet good atmospheres seldom materialise spontaneously. They result from deliberate actions, where every team member plays a part in shaping an uplifting culture.

One immediate practice is showing regular acknowledgment of colleagues' efforts. Whether it is a manager praising an employee's quick problem-solving or a teammate sending a note of thanks for someone's support, this recognition bolsters morale. Even a concise message like "Thank you for stepping up earlier" fosters a sense of belonging. It signals to your colleagues that their actions do not go unnoticed. Repeated acts of appreciation gradually set a friendly tone, prompting others to respond in kind.

Open communication is another building block. Encourage honesty in how feedback is offered, focusing on constructive advice rather than criticism. If a plan does not work, phrase your comments as, "We might explore a different approach," or "I see potential in a revision to this section." When your coworkers trust that no one will belittle them for missteps, they become more willing to experiment with ideas. This

The Workplace: Building Positive Professional Connections

open exchange, free of fear, fuels innovation and team growth.

Psychological safety is vital. Team members should feel comfortable voicing concerns or critiques without risking backlash. If someone identifies a serious flaw in a strategy, they need to be heard rather than dismissed. Once psychological safety grows, people share more openly, saving the group from expensive errors or oversights. This fosters loyalty since employees see that the group values truth over politics or preserving appearances.

Flexibility in how work is done can also bolster positivity. If feasible, flexible work hours or remote options enable employees to manage personal responsibilities while still meeting professional standards. If your company structure does not permit full flexibility, small adaptations, like letting a colleague come in later if they had an urgent errand, still reflect that the business respects personal lives. Feeling that your employer considers your human needs often makes you more committed and energetic.

Team-building activities further unify people. These need not be extravagant. Even a casual lunch out or a monthly brainstorming session free from strict agendas can strengthen interpersonal bonds. Lighthearted moments release tension, helping colleagues see each other's personalities beyond job roles. This sense of camaraderie can later prove invaluable. If conflict arises, it is easier to remember shared good times and approach each other with empathy.

Leadership style plays a critical role. Managers and supervisors, in particular, set the cultural tone. If they lead with compassion and fairness, encouraging open dialogue, employees tend to mirror that behaviour. Conversely, autocratic or dismissive leadership fosters fear and resentment. By embodying consistency in words and deeds, leaders reassure teams that positivity is not a mere buzzword but a lived principle.

Therefore, cultivating a positive environment goes beyond company slogans. It is a series of mindful choices: recognising each other's achievements, engaging in open conversations, encouraging honest feedback, and being flexible when possible. Over time, these actions accumulate into an office climate where trust blossoms, stress is more manageable, and colleagues genuinely care about mutual success. This synergy is the hallmark of an environment that not only helps you thrive but also inspires you to contribute your best.

Setting Boundaries with Colleagues and Superiors

While collaboration is crucial in a professional environment, personal boundaries remain essential. You might have friendly relationships with co-workers or find your manager quite approachable, but that does not negate your right to privacy or time off. Boundaries define what you can handle while preserving your mental and emotional health. Without them, your workload can balloon, or you may find yourself constantly anxious or overextended.

Begin by identifying areas where you feel the need for clearer lines. It might be your time, such as resisting after-hours calls that interrupt family life. It could be personal information, deciding that details about your romantic life or finances are not subjects you share with colleagues. You also want to notice if certain tasks keep falling on your plate,

The Workplace: Building Positive Professional Connections

even if they surpass your role. Noticing these patterns lets you formulate a boundary plan.

Communication is the next step. Politely but assertively mention your limits. For instance, if a colleague emails you late at night, expecting an immediate response, you can clarify, "I handle non-urgent messages the next business day." Alternatively, if your supervisor loads you with extra tasks, you might say, "I currently have X, Y, and Z. Which one should take priority, given time constraints?" This approach does not read as refusal but as a practical request for guidance. You subtly show that your plate is full without sounding defiant.

Boundaries also apply to emotional topics. Perhaps a co-worker frequently vents about their personal life, expecting you to act as a counsellor. If you feel drained, you can respond kindly: "I sense this is difficult for you. I do care, but I need to stay focused on my tasks now. If you need deeper support, maybe you should speak to a professional, or we can chat briefly after hours if that suits both of us." This balanced response acknowledges compassion but prevents you from absorbing constant negativity at your desk.

Consistently reinforcing boundaries cements them. If you allow one exception, like responding to a midnight text about a non-urgent matter, you risk inviting more of the same. By remaining consistent, colleagues or superiors learn what to expect. Over time, they adapt. Should they pressure you, remind them gently but firmly of your stance. You could say, "As mentioned, I am offline during weekends," or "I am at full capacity; I cannot take on additional work unless we adjust existing tasks." This repetition might feel awkward, but it protects your well-being.

Finally, do not confuse boundaries with a lack of team spirit. You can be collaborative and friendly while honouring your limits. The aim is not to erect walls but to define the space in which you can be most effective. If a manager or colleague dismisses your boundary, stay calm. Restate your points, or if that fails, escalate to HR or another relevant channel. The underlying belief is that you deserve respect, and a workplace that regularly violates personal boundaries may not be the right environment for you long-term. By standing up for your needs politely, you lay the groundwork for healthier interactions, ensuring you contribute productively without compromising your sense of self.

Recognising and Dealing with Workplace Energy Vampires

In professional settings, you often encounter individuals who consistently sap your motivation. Dubbed workplace "Energy Vampires," they may arrive each morning with a litany of complaints or generate tension with every project they touch. Their negative patterns disrupt morale, derail productivity, and leave you feeling tired. While you might not choose to associate with them personally, your job obligations may require regular interaction, so learning to manage them is key.

Spotting these Energy Vampires starts with noticing how you feel after an exchange. Do you sense a drop in optimism or a sudden surge of stress? Some colleagues might project pessimism onto every task, or speak endlessly about personal woes without seeking genuine solutions. Others foster drama, stirring conflict between team members to draw attention. By identifying these traits, you can mentally

The Workplace: Building Positive Professional Connections

prepare to protect your energy during upcoming interactions.

Setting limits politely but firmly is a practical first line of defence. If a colleague corners you with a continuous rant about office policies, you might say, "I hear your concerns, but I have deadlines to focus on. Perhaps we can address this at a more convenient time." This approach acknowledges their feelings yet signals you are not an endless venting post. Over time, they might reduce attempts to drag you into their negativity or choose a more willing audience.

Selective listening also helps. Instead of engaging with every complaint, identify the points that truly affect your work. You can respond to those and sidestep the rest. For example, if a co-worker complains about the boss's leadership style, ignore the personal jabs. Instead, address any relevant points, such as how it affects your team's task prioritisation. It steers the conversation into constructive territory, preventing you from being swamped by gossip or moaning.

Emotional detachment is another tool. When confronted with an Energy Vampire, you can visualise a mental barrier that keeps their negativity from permeating your emotional state. If they lash out or exaggerate problems, remind yourself that these are their perceptions, not facts. This technique allows you to remain courteous without internalising their gloomy worldview. Later, if you feel a residue of stress, take a short break, a sip of water, or a quick stretch to reclaim a calmer mindset.

If the negativity escalates to bullying or toxic conduct, escalate responsibly. Document examples, note dates or times, and consult with your manager or HR if appropriate.

Tolerating abusive behaviour is never part of a normal job description. By addressing it through official channels, you protect yourself and potentially help colleagues facing similar pressure. Good organisations want to maintain a healthy culture and will intervene where possible.

Finally, balance is crucial. Surround yourself with positive influences at work to offset the drain from any Energy Vampires. If you have colleagues who share your proactive attitude, spend your breaks chatting with them. Seek mentors or supportive team members who energise you. This approach helps you hold onto your positivity, reaffirming that not all corners of the workplace revolve around negativity. Over time, by practising these strategies, you reduce the impact of Energy Vampires on your daily routine, preserving a more vibrant, self-assured stance in your professional world.

Building Collaborative Relationships

Work can sometimes feel competitive, with each person vying for recognition or promotion. Yet collaboration remains crucial for achieving ambitious objectives. When individuals join forces, the results usually outshine what anyone could accomplish alone. If you adopt a cooperative mindset, you not only enhance productivity but also create meaningful relationships that make daily tasks more gratifying.

Begin by highlighting shared objectives. If your team is tasked with launching a product or streamlining processes, underline that success hinges on collective effort. Rather than fixating on personal credit, encourage a mindset of unity: "Let us see how we can bring our talents together to hit these targets." This approach shifts perspective away from "I must outdo my colleagues" toward "We can accomplish more as a group." As soon as people sense that everyone is working for a mutual cause, they become more open to contributing ideas.

Communication in collaborative work goes beyond formal meetings. Regular check-ins are beneficial, whether quick stand-ups or casual updates. Keep them brief but inclusive, letting each member speak. Ask about obstacles or resources they may need. By providing a consistent platform for discussion, you remove guesswork about who is handling what. This transparency discourages confusion that can breed mistrust or duplication of tasks.

Respect for different styles and strengths underpins successful collaboration. Some colleagues excel at creative brainstorming, while others thrive in meticulous planning or final execution. Rather than insisting your method is best, you can harness the variety of skills available. If a teammate loves detail-oriented tasks, let them handle data analysis or scheduling. If someone is an excellent communicator, trust them with client presentations. Aligning tasks with strengths ensures the team runs fluidly and fosters personal satisfaction.

Conflict is normal when diverse minds work together, so approach disagreements with a solution-focused attitude. Suppose two team members clash over how to allocate a budget. You might step in with a calm statement: "I see you have different strategies. Let us list the pros and cons of each, then decide collectively." This approach values every viewpoint while preventing a heated argument. Over time, handling conflicts constructively cultivates a sense of unity and mutual respect, even among individuals who see things differently.

Support each other's growth. If you master a software tool, offer a small training session so others can pick it up. If a colleague wants to improve public speaking, encourage them to lead the next meeting. By freely sharing expertise, you break the notion that knowledge is power to be guarded. Instead, knowledge becomes a community resource, improving overall efficiency. People are more inclined to share their knowledge in return, making the environment cooperative rather than combative.

Lastly, celebrate team victories. Whether you complete a challenging project under budget or reach new performance metrics, take a moment to acknowledge everyone's input. This could be as simple as a group email praising the effort or a coffee gathering to toast the accomplishment. Acknowledgement cements the bond and fosters a sense of pride. Everyone sees tangible evidence that cooperative relationships yield rewarding outcomes. When collaboration is woven into the daily culture, morale rises and the workplace becomes a place of dynamic synergy, rather than a battleground of clashing egos.

Nurturing Mentorships and Support Networks

Mentorship can be a game-changer in your professional journey. Whether you are a newcomer seeking guidance or a seasoned professional looking to share your insights, mentorship fosters growth for both parties. By nurturing supportive relationships within your organisation or industry, you elevate your skills, expand your horizons, and help others do the same.

Starting with yourself, reflect on what you aim to learn or develop. If you desire stronger leadership skills or deeper

The Workplace: Building Positive Professional Connections

knowledge of a specific field, identify potential mentors who exemplify those traits. Approach them politely, perhaps with an email that briefly introduces your background and your admiration for their expertise. Let them know you are open to any tips or short meetings, making it clear you respect their schedule. Many individuals, having benefited from mentors themselves, are pleased to guide newcomers who show genuine enthusiasm and humility.

Once you have found a mentor, establish a clear structure for your sessions. You might meet monthly for an hour, discussing your recent achievements, hurdles, and queries. Keeping notes helps you track progress, so you come prepared each time rather than repeating old questions. Show gratitude for your mentor's time by following up on any suggestions or resources they provide. This respect for their input demonstrates your commitment to making the most of the relationship.

Mentorship also works in reverse. Even if you are not a top executive, you can mentor those less experienced in certain areas. If a new colleague struggles with a software you have mastered, offer to teach them. This not only helps them settle in but also bolsters your leadership capacity. You learn to convey knowledge clearly and empathise with their learning curve. Over time, you build a reputation as someone who invests in others' success, enhancing your standing in the team or broader network.

Support networks extend mentorship's spirit to a collective. These can be formal groups within your company, like a peer support cluster or a cross-departmental club, or an online community of professionals in your field. Within these networks, individuals share advice, job leads, or problem-solving strategies. If your job environment does not offer such groups, consider initiating a small gathering yourself. A monthly forum to trade ideas or a digital chat can suffice. It might be as simple as inviting peers to share best practices or lessons learned.

Another angle involves external organisations or industry associations that frequently host workshops or conferences. Attending these events expands your circle beyond the confines of your workplace. You might meet potential mentors or mentees from diverse backgrounds, broadening your insight into different corporate cultures or technical approaches. Over time, these contacts evolve into a robust support network you can rely on for referrals, knowledge exchange, or moral support if you navigate a job transition.

The ultimate benefit is a collective ethos of helping each other thrive. When you invest in mentorship and supportive networks, you become part of a community where knowledge is not hoarded but distributed widely. Everyone lifts each other, forging bonds that often outlast specific roles or companies. This synergy improves your expertise and fosters friendships that can last a lifetime, offering a sense of belonging in a competitive professional world. If the wider workplace spirit ever wanes, these networks remain, reminding you that your growth is both an individual and a shared endeavour.

Balancing Professionalism and Personal Connection

A healthy workplace often blends a professional demeanour with genuine warmth. You might share small bits of your personal life, celebrate achievements, and exchange light

The Workplace: Building Positive Professional Connections

banter, all while upholding the standards of your role. However, it can be tricky to find that sweet spot. Be too distant and you risk appearing aloof; become too familiar and professionalism can suffer. Striking the right balance is an ongoing practice, shaped by your organisation's culture and your personal comfort levels.

Professionalism ensures tasks are completed efficiently, deadlines are met, and codes of conduct are upheld. It also fosters respect. If you handle yourself in a consistent, courteous manner, you earn colleagues' trust, showing that you can separate personal moods from your responsibilities. For example, you might greet co-workers politely even if you feel tired, or refrain from outbursts when a project hits snags. This sense of self-control builds confidence that you can handle pressure without unleashing negativity on everyone else.

However, total formality can cause an atmosphere of stiffness, where employees feel they must always stand on ceremony. Personal connection helps soften edges. Simple gestures, like acknowledging someone's hobby or inquiring about a colleague's holiday, bring warmth to daily interactions. These moments reveal a shared humanity, making the workspace more engaging than a purely transactional environment. They might appear small, but they show that you see your co-workers as complete people, not just roles or job titles.

Choosing what personal details to share requires discernment. Certain topics, like deeply personal struggles, explicit political stances, or intimate relationship details, might not be appropriate in a team setting, especially if it distracts from the job or causes contention. Nonetheless, you can mention general personal experiences. Maybe you talk about a recent weekend getaway, an amusing incident with your pet, or a skill you are learning outside work. This level of sharing can spark conversation without blurring lines too much.

Listening also supports that balance. Ask your co-workers how their weekend went, or congratulate them on personal milestones, like completing a charity run. If someone is comfortable, they might share photos or stories, building a friendly rapport. Meanwhile, remain sensitive to cues; if they answer tersely, they may prefer to keep their personal life private. Respecting these boundaries ensures no one feels pressured to reveal more than they wish.

Social events outside office hours can further fuse personal bonds with professional respect. A casual dinner or team-building activity breaks standard hierarchies for a while, letting you see managers and peers in a more relaxed context. Yet, maintain composure. Overindulgence or overly familiar behaviour can sabotage your reputation. Enjoy the more light-hearted environment, but remember you are still representing yourself as a member of the team.

By combining professional etiquette with genuine friendliness, you create an environment where everyone feels seen and appreciated, yet understands the boundaries that keep things productive and respectful. As you refine this skill, you become an example to others, promoting both efficiency and cordiality. In the end, your co-workers will note that you handle tasks diligently while demonstrating kindness, a balance that often leads to stronger collaborations and a more pleasant workspace for everyone involved.

Leading with Empathy: The Role of Leadership in Workplace Energy

Leaders profoundly shape how employees feel in the workplace. A manager or supervisor who leads with empathy can foster positivity that boosts morale and encourages excellence. In contrast, a leader who relies on intimidation or indifference can create an atmosphere of tension or fear. If you hold any leadership role, whether as a team head or project coordinator, adopting empathetic strategies elevates both your results and team satisfaction.

Empathy begins with attentiveness. Keep an eye on your team's moods and performance. If someone who usually excels seems withdrawn, do not dismiss it as laziness. A private chat might reveal stress at home or burnout. Approaching them calmly, "I noticed you have been quieter; is anything going on?" can spark an honest conversation. Even if you cannot fully solve their personal issues, acknowledging them can lessen feelings of isolation. This personal concern sends a powerful message: "You matter here."

Leaders who practise empathy also stay open to feedback. Instead of commanding from above, they invite opinions: "How do you feel about our current process? Any ideas for making it smoother?" Colleagues often spot inefficiencies or burdens that the leader might not see. By encouraging candid input, you reduce frustration and build trust. People who feel heard are more likely to engage wholeheartedly, spurring innovation. They realise the leader genuinely seeks better ways of working, not merely top-down directives.

Conflict resolution also benefits from empathetic leadership. If two team members clash, an empathetic leader sits them down for a fair discussion, guiding them to articulate their frustrations in a constructive manner. You might ask each person how the conflict is affecting their tasks, and what they hope for. By listening carefully and reframing accusations into shared objectives, you reduce blame and encourage them to find a solution that works for both sides. The result is not a forced compromise, but a deeper understanding that fosters lasting cooperation.

At times, empathy includes practicality. Suppose a team member has to juggle a family crisis. Adjusting their workload temporarily or offering flexible hours might enable them to manage both responsibilities. While you cannot accommodate every personal request, gestures of support where feasible show genuine regard. Employees rarely forget kindness they receive during tough periods. Later, they often reciprocate with loyalty and extra effort when projects demand it.

Recognising achievements in a thoughtful way is another hallmark of empathetic leadership. Whether it is a team success or an individual accomplishment, praising specific qualities fosters self-esteem and motivation. Rather than saying, "Good job," detail what impressed you: "Your attention to detail in those charts helped the entire team spot crucial data." Such recognition affirms their contributions on a personal level, forging a more engaged workforce.

By leading with empathy, you set an emotional tone that others follow. People often emulate a leader's method of handling stress or conflict. If they see compassion in your approach, they are likely to replicate it in their own interactions. Over time, the entire culture shifts toward one of mutual support. Productivity tends to increase as employees feel valued rather than merely tasked. Moreover, staff turnover can dip, saving the company resources while preserving institutional knowledge. Ultimately, empathy in leadership is not about leniency. It is about uplifting your team so they can operate at their best while feeling respected and emotionally secure.

The Impact of Work-Life Balance on Professional Relationships

When you are fulfilled outside your job, it often reflects positively on how you behave with colleagues. Conversely, a lack of work-life balance can drive irritability, fatigue, and reduced productivity, which seeps into professional relationships. Creating boundaries around your personal time benefits not just you but also your peers. In this section, you will see how adjusting your work-life habits can elevate your workplace interactions.

An unbalanced lifestyle might leave you perpetually stressed, carrying that tension into meetings. You might snap at a co-worker for small mishaps or struggle to concentrate on group projects. If your evenings are consumed by replying to work emails, you rarely switch off mentally, leading to drained morale. This depletion can make any interpersonal friction heavier. Over time, your colleagues might sense that you are burned out, influencing their own morale as well.

Conversely, when you have space for personal hobbies, family time, or rest, you are generally more present at work. You are less likely to take out frustration on others, and your energy levels remain consistent. You can approach tasks with clarity, show patience, and encourage thoughtful dialogue. This calmer disposition sets a constructive tone for your team. While you might not have perfect equilibrium every day, even moderate improvements in scheduling or self-care can yield noticeable shifts in workplace relations.

Establishing and respecting personal boundaries is a key strategy. If your job often bleeds into nights and weekends, have honest discussions with your manager or co-workers about realistic workloads. Even if certain deadlines remain rigid, maybe you can negotiate flexi-time or a day to work from home occasionally. These small changes remind your colleagues that you respect your well-being and request that they do likewise. When you are not always reachable 24/7, you might feel more rested, enabling you to be sharper during working hours.

Another element is mindful personal downtime. If you do have time off, avoid checking work notifications or responding to group chats about minor issues. Let yourself fully disengage. By returning to the office mentally recharged, you bring a fresher perspective. This approach benefits the group, as you can provide better solutions and hold a more positive demeanour. In a sense, stepping away from work lets you come back stronger, which is beneficial to everyone you interact with.

Management also plays a part in encouraging work-life balance. If you hold a leadership role, model respectful hours. If staff see you emailing them late at night, they might believe they must do the same. Adjusting your own habits can shape cultural norms. If your workplace sees value in mental breaks, staff can deal with everyday pressure more gracefully, minimising needless friction. Over time, the environment becomes more empathetic, and team members feel safer addressing issues like exhaustion or time conflicts.

Ultimately, achieving a reasonable work-life balance is not just about personal satisfaction. It also cements healthier professional relationships. You protect your well-being, reduce the risk of conflict caused by stress, and demonstrate that a good employee is not one who is always "on call" but one who is consistently effective and collegial when they are at work. That balance can be contagious, paving the way for a supportive climate where everyone acknowledges that employees are humans first, professionals second.

Transforming Conflict into Collaboration

Disagreements at work are unavoidable, given that different departments, personalities, and opinions must collaborate daily. However, conflicts need not always be destructive. If you and your colleagues handle them constructively, conflict can be turned into progress. Instead of undermining relationships, disagreements can lead to more innovative solutions when managed respectfully.

Begin by addressing conflict as soon as you sense it is brewing. Do not wait for resentments to balloon into larger issues. Summon the involved parties if you have the authority to do so, and clarify that you want to find a common ground. Encourage each person to present their perspective calmly. If you are a peer, you might initiate a private conversation with the colleague you disagree with, stating, "We seem to view this differently; I would like to understand your reasoning better." Prompt, measured intervention contains potential damage.

Active listening is crucial at this point. Allow each side to explain their stance fully without interruption. Reflect back what they say with statements like, "You feel overshadowed in decisions, correct?" or "You believe the timeline is not realistic?" This approach ensures everyone feels heard. Once each viewpoint is on the table, you can pinpoint the exact root of the conflict, which often differs from initial assumptions. For instance, you might discover that the real issue is not the project's direction but a lack of communication about deadlines.

Next, move into brainstorming solutions. Ask, "How can we meet your need for more clarity while also achieving the required outcomes?" This question reframes tension from confrontation to collaboration. You create a sense that all voices matter in shaping the path forward. If the conflict involves multiple departments, consider having a neutral mediator present. They keep discussions on track, prompting constructive language and fair opportunities for each side to speak.

Focus on the shared objectives. Even if your roles differ, you likely share an overarching mission, such as delivering a project on time or enhancing customer satisfaction. Emphasise this bigger picture: "We both want this product to succeed. Let us see which approach best serves that aim." By shifting attention away from personal pride or departmental competition, you remind everyone of the unity behind the project.

Once a compromise or a blended solution emerges, clarify the next steps. Who will do what, and by when? Ensure no confusion remains about responsibilities. Summarise the agreement: "We have agreed that the marketing team will test the new strategy, and the development team will modify the interface as needed. We will reconvene next Wednesday to evaluate the results." This step cements accountability, preventing any subsequent confusion.

Finally, follow up after implementing the resolution. If tensions linger, another quick check-in can reaffirm trust. Over time, you might notice the team grows more adept at handling disputes. Instead of seeing conflict as a threat, you acknowledge that differences often lead to growth when managed properly. Co-workers who previously clashed might emerge with a renewed respect for each other's expertise, forging collaborative bonds that stand the test of future disagreements. By transforming conflict into collaboration, you not only solve immediate problems but also foster an environment in which honesty and respect prevail.

In Conclusion

You have explored how emotional intelligence, empathy-driven leadership, and clear boundaries all shape a constructive workplace atmosphere. Whether you are managing challenging colleagues or building collaborative networks, every interaction can elevate morale and productivity when approached with respect and transparency. Your professional life is more than tasks and deadlines. It is also about forging respectful, energising relationships that improve the entire working sphere.

Now that you have gained insights into the professional realm, the final chapters turn inward again, focusing on self-connection and the wider impact of positive relationships. Get ready to align your personal journey with the way you show up for others, discovering how your internal balance supports all your connections in a transformative ripple effect.

Chapter 9

Self-Connection: The Foundation of All Relationships

Every relationship you nurture in life reflects how deeply you know and care for yourself. When you are disconnected from your true feelings, it becomes harder to sense how you affect others. If you do not respect your own boundaries, you often overlook them in your interactions. This chapter reveals why self-connection is indispensable for forming meaningful bonds. You will see how self-awareness and self-care translate into stronger, more empathic relationships and how aligning with your innermost values makes every connection more authentic.

Through each subheading, you will explore practices ranging from mindfulness and self-reflection to letting go of your inner critic. You will learn to spot the personal energy you carry into interactions, ensuring you remain in harmony with the person you strive to be. By the end, you will appreciate that self-connection is not self-indulgence but the bedrock of healthy external relationships. It grants you clarity and calm, helping you engage with others on a balanced, more compassionate level.

Understanding Your Inner Energy Landscape

Much of life's stress arises when your internal energy runs low or becomes misdirected. If you move through your day without pausing to notice how you feel, you can accumulate

Connections

tension or negativity. In turn, that unsettled energy colours your interactions. By recognising your inner energy landscape, you gain greater command over how you show up for loved ones, colleagues, and everyone else you encounter.

This landscape includes emotional states like joy, anxiety, and hope, but it also comprises subtler undercurrents, your mental chatter and bodily tension. Perhaps you have occasional aches that reflect unresolved strain or a nagging restlessness that surfaces only when you attempt to relax. These signals matter. They tell you which parts f your life need attention. For instance, if you notice you become edgy each time a particular name crosses your phone, it might indicate tension with that individual or dread of their demands.

A tool for gaining awareness is the daily check-in. Each morning or evening, devote a few minutes to assessing whether you feel energised, fatigued, uplifted, or heavy-hearted. Note the parts of your body that feel tense. Maybe your shoulders are tight, or your stomach churns. Link these sensations to possible causes. If your shoulders always tense after reading certain emails, you might look into strategies for addressing that source of stress or for adjusting your own response. Over time, these observations help you form a map of your emotional triggers and calm points.

Equally important is identifying what recharges you. Everybody has unique sources of renewal. Some people need an hour of solitary time, reading or journaling. Others crave a brisk walk or a quick chat with a positive friend. By exploring different options, like painting, a warm bath, or

Self-Connection: The Foundation of All Relationships

listening to soothing music, you discover which ones effectively refresh your spirit. Once you pinpoint these outlets, you can more intentionally use them when you feel your energy waning.

Occasionally, you may need deeper reflection. If persistent sadness or anxiety lingers despite self-care efforts, it might hint at unresolved trauma or ongoing conflict. Rather than ignoring it, recognise the possibility that professional help could expedite your healing. Seeing a counsellor or therapist does not mean you are broken; it shows you want to clarify hidden aspects of your inner landscape and learn better coping tools.

As you become more adept at reading your energy patterns, you will find your relationships benefit. If you sense irritability brewing from a hectic day, you can briefly breathe, stretch, or step outside for a moment before meeting a friend or partner. This act of self-regulation spares them from your frustration and spares you from regrets about snapping unnecessarily. You start creating a buffer between your mood and your interactions so you can communicate kindly, even under stress.

Ultimately, understanding your inner energy landscape is a journey of self-observation and gentle adjustment. It allows you to approach each day with a clearer sense of your emotional reserves, recognising when to slow down, when to reach out for support, and when to extend empathy to others. By tending to your emotional soil, you make sure that what grows outward, your words and gestures, reflects a grounded, authentic self.

The Importance of Self-Love and Self-Respect

Connections

Self-love can sound clichéd, but it is actually the cornerstone of a healthy, balanced life. It is the ability to see yourself as worthy of kindness, to acknowledge your strengths while forgiving your flaws. Self-respect expands on that foundation, reminding you that you have the right to decide how others treat you. Together, these qualities shape how you navigate both daily interactions and long-term bonds.

At its core, self-love is not about self-indulgence. It is about recognising that your physical and emotional well-being matter. When you care for yourself by eating well, resting adequately, and nurturing a positive mindset, you give yourself the best chance to be fully present and supportive toward others. Neglecting these acts can lead to exhaustion or resentment, which easily spills into your relationships. If you fail to treat yourself with care, you cannot maintain a consistent, uplifting presence for friends, family, or colleagues.

Self-respect translates these values into boundaries. If a friend frequently oversteps your limits, self-respect motivates you to speak up. You might say, "I appreciate your concern, but I need space to handle this on my own." Similarly, in a job context, it might mean pushing back if you are assigned tasks beyond your role or forced to endure disrespect. You can politely but firmly clarify what you will or will not tolerate. Being assertive does not mean being harsh or arrogant. It means preserving your mental health and dignity.

One major hurdle to self-love is past conditioning. Perhaps you grew up equating self-appreciation with vanity or were taught that focusing on yourself is selfish. Overcoming these

Self-Connection: The Foundation of All Relationships

views involves reframing your mindset. Giving yourself permission to thrive does not ignore others' needs. In fact, a well-cared-for person typically has more capacity to empathise, guide, and care for others. If you burn out, you lose the chance to share your gifts fully.

To develop self-love, begin with small affirmations: "I treat myself with kindness and patience," or "I value who I am, flaws included." These statements might feel awkward initially, but they retrain your inner narrative. You might also note daily achievements or moments you handled well. Listing them reminds you of your strengths. Such reflections ground you, especially if self-criticism creeps in. Over time, you adopt a friendlier attitude toward yourself, which fosters resilience when times get rough.

Self-respect often involves stepping out of people-pleasing habits. If you constantly alter your opinions or decisions to earn approval, you erode your own sense of worth. Start by asserting small preferences, like choosing which restaurant to dine in with friends or saying no to extra tasks when your schedule is full. Each act of self-assertion cultivates a healthier dynamic, where people learn to respect your boundaries. In turn, you feel more at peace because you are not betraying yourself for the sake of external harmony.

Ultimately, by upholding self-love and self-respect, you create an emotional framework that encourages growth and genuine connection. People around you witness that you care for yourself and that you handle your life with integrity. Far from alienating anyone, it often attracts those who appreciate your confidence. In relationships, you no longer rely on others to fill emotional voids that only you can fill. Instead, you stand as a complete individual, ready to share your life with equals rather than submerging your identity to suit someone else's vision.

Mindfulness: Being Present with Yourself

Mindfulness is about being truly present in the moment rather than letting your mind churn over regrets or future anxieties. When applied to self-connection, it means deliberately focusing on your thoughts and emotions as they arise without scolding or ignoring them. By embracing mindfulness in daily life, you develop a calmer, clearer vantage point from which to understand yourself, setting a foundation for more meaningful external bonds.

This practice can start with small, purposeful steps. For instance, as you wake up, resist grabbing your phone. Spend a minute noticing how your body feels, how your breath flows in and out. If you detect stiffness or restlessness, take a few gentle stretches or a moment to breathe more deeply. This short routine signals your intention for the day, reminding you that you have the power to tune in before external demands flood your consciousness.

Mindful breathing is a popular technique. Select a short period, two to five minutes, and focus solely on your breath. Inhale for a set count, pause briefly and then exhale. If your mind wanders, that is normal. Gently bring your focus back to your breathing. Over time, this habit teaches you to notice mental clutter without getting lost in it. You gain a skill that can be used in stressful settings, too, like a tense meeting or an argument with a loved one. You can centre yourself in a matter of seconds, keeping your composure.

You can extend mindfulness to eating. Rather than rushing through lunch while checking emails, concentrate on

Self-Connection: The Foundation of All Relationships

flavours, textures, and your body's signals of hunger and satisfaction. This approach can improve your digestion and transform a mundane activity into a grounding experience. Mindful eating also encourages gratitude for the nourishment you receive. As you give your meal your full attention, you anchor your awareness in the present, refreshing your mind before returning to tasks.

Beyond physical tasks, mindfulness also helps you recognise emotional patterns. Suppose you feel anxiety creeping in when you are about to speak with your manager. Instead of trying to shut it down, you might pause, acknowledge that your heart rate has quickened, and label the emotion as nervousness. Accepting it without judgement often reduces its intensity. You can then proceed more calmly, remembering that a bit of nerves is natural and does not define you.

At first, you might find mindfulness challenging. Modern life bombards you with notifications, errands, and distractions. However, each small moment of conscious presence accumulates. Even if you practise mindfulness for brief intervals, you begin to notice improved focus, greater emotional resilience, and a steadier sense of well-being. You respond more thoughtfully to unexpected events because you are not as entangled in past regrets or future worries.

By continually bringing your attention back to the present, you root yourself in reality rather than ruminations. This mindful stance fosters genuine self-connection. You learn to detect minor shifts in your mood or energy so you can handle them gently rather than allowing them to erupt uncontrollably. Ultimately, the calm you cultivate in yourself reflects outward, letting you engage in life's interactions from a stable, grounded place. That solidity stands as the bedrock of all other connections, be they familial, romantic, or professional.

Managing Your Energy: Techniques and Practices

Your energy is a delicate resource influenced by emotional states, physical health, and the demands of daily life. If you feel rushed or depleted, it becomes harder to remain positive around others. Therefore, managing your energy is as vital as organising your schedule or finances. By adopting certain techniques and practices, you maintain a steady emotional reservoir that benefits both you and your relationships.

One helpful method is time-blocking for self-care. Pick portions of your week, however brief, solely dedicated to activities that revitalise you. It could be half an hour for a quiet hobby or a walk in fresh air. Once scheduled, treat it as you would a professional meeting- non-negotiable and crucial for your well-being. When you see it in your diary, you are less likely to brush it aside for other tasks. This approach ensures you do not go days without focusing on your own equilibrium.

Meditation or breathing exercises can also anchor your energy. Even a few minutes spent focusing on your breath helps you let go of mental clutter. Similarly, progressive muscle relaxation, where you tense and release muscle groups in sequence, reduces tension. Over time, these habits recalibrate your stress responses, teaching your body and mind to shift from high alert to calm more fluidly. You avoid the pitfall of living in perpetual hustle mode.

Self-Connection: The Foundation of All Relationships

Physical exercise plays its part in energy management. This does not need to be extreme. A brisk daily walk or short yoga session can stimulate your body's endorphins, giving you a lift in mood. Movement also helps flush out pent-up anxiety or restlessness from sitting at a desk too long. When you keep consistent with mild exercise, you often sleep more deeply, which in turn replenishes your energy for the next day's social or professional commitments.

Mindful boundaries around technology also matter. Constant notifications can chip away at your focus and mental clarity, leaving you frazzled. Consider silencing phone alerts for set periods or using apps that limit time on social media. If your job requires you to be online often, designate offline blocks, even if they are short. During these times, you can read a physical book or practise a hobby that engages you without screens. This periodic disconnect keeps your mind from overload, helping you return to your daily tasks refreshed.

Pay attention to your nutritional and sleep patterns, too. If you skip meals or rely heavily on sugary snacks, your energy levels spike and crash rapidly, clouding your mental state. Aim for balanced meals with protein and healthy fats, and keep hydrated with sufficient water. Meanwhile, a proper bedtime routine, like avoiding bright screens before bed, improves sleep quality. Adequate rest underpins your daily mood and resilience, forming a bedrock of stable energy.

Finally, monitoring your progress can help you refine these techniques. Jot down which strategies work best: Perhaps you realise short midday walks drastically raise your afternoon energy or that a ten-minute digital detox at night improves your morning mood. Adjust accordingly, letting your body and mind guide you. By systematically managing your energy, you not only feel better internally but also create a more consistent, positive presence for those around you. Rather than running on empty and snapping at loved ones, you engage from a place of balanced vitality.

The Power of Solitude: Recharging Your Inner Battery

Modern life teems with noise and demands, from social media pings to professional tasks. You might feel guilty for wanting alone time, especially if others view it as antisocial. Yet solitude stands as a vital component for recharging your inner reserves and clarifying your perspective. By granting yourself these intervals of quiet, you regain a sense of who you are beyond external roles and obligations.

Solitude differs from loneliness. Loneliness arises when you yearn for human contact but cannot find it. Solitude is a choice to be with yourself, often leading to a calm introspection that fosters creative insights and stress relief. It can be as modest as choosing to have your morning cup of tea in silence, looking out a window rather than scrolling through your phone. This short ritual allows your mind to settle, washing away overnight worries or impending day pressures.

A longer period of solitude, such as a weekend retreat or a dedicated hour of reading without distractions, can reveal deeper mental layers. You might notice unresolved emotions or dreams that never had the space to surface. Reflecting in a journal or simply letting your mind wander can spark fresh ideas. Artists, writers, and entrepreneurs often champion solitary moments as the cradle of innovation. Away from the crowd's opinions, you tap into your unique voice.

Self-Connection: The Foundation of All Relationships

Solitude also helps you break cycles of people-pleasing. In group settings, you may adapt your preferences to maintain harmony, eventually losing track of your true inclinations. By stepping away briefly, you reconnect with your preferences and feelings. When you rejoin social spheres, you carry a clearer sense of self, enhancing authenticity in your interactions.

Setting boundaries around solitude is essential. Loved ones or housemates might see your desire for quiet time as a rejection. Communicate that it is about recharging, not about pushing them away. If necessary, schedule it explicitly: "I plan to have a silent hour each evening to wind down," or "I will go for a solitary walk each Sunday." When repeated consistently, these sessions become part of your routine. People adapt, usually respecting your need once they see the benefits to your mood and well-being.

The environment you select for solitude also matters. A bustling living room with a TV running might hamper the very calm you seek. If you cannot find peace at home, consider a local park, a quiet café at non-peak hours, or an unused conference room at your workplace after typical hours. Even a parked car can provide a little oasis, switch off the engine, open the window slightly, and take a brief lull to gather your thoughts.

In short, solitude is not escapism. It is a proactive choice to pause and let your internal battery recharge. Rather than feeling you must always be "on," entertaining or managing others, you allow your mind to settle, your emotions to regulate, and your imagination to rekindle. Returning from solitude, you are better equipped to interact positively and respond thoughtfully, making your presence more valuable to yourself and everyone around you.

Aligning Your Actions with Your Values

There may be times in life when your behaviour and your deeper values do not align. Perhaps you say you cherish honesty, yet find yourself shading the truth in social or professional settings. Or you hold family as a priority but rarely set aside quality time for them. This disconnect can leave you uneasy, as though part of you knows something is amiss. Aligning actions with values is a key step in self-connection, granting you a grounded sense of integrity and reducing internal conflict.

Begin by clarifying your core values. Ask yourself what principles genuinely guide your life. Is it compassion, creativity, humility, or personal growth? Write them down in a place you can revisit often. These values help you decide how to spend your time and which relationships to cultivate. For instance, if kindness is essential to you, volunteering or daily acts of generosity might become part of your routine, while malicious gossip or persistent negativity becomes less tolerable.

Next, evaluate your current lifestyle. If you claim health is a priority but skip exercise and rely on junky snacks, notice that mismatch. Rather than feeling guilt, frame it as an opportunity: "I see I have neglected this area. What consistent steps can I take to bridge the gap?" That mindset fosters growth. Similarly, if you prize knowledge, challenge yourself to read or research a bit each day. Over time, deliberate efforts turn a vague ideal, "I respect learning", into a lived reality.

Self-Connection: The Foundation of All Relationships

Everyday decisions can reinforce or undermine your values. Suppose you value environmental stewardship yet find it inconvenient to recycle or reduce plastic. You could take baby steps: carry reusable bags, invest in a water filter to cut plastic bottles, or choose public transport occasionally. These acts, though small, symbolise commitment. They remind you that your words match your deeds. That coherence boosts self-confidence and personal clarity.

Value alignment also matters in choosing relationships or activities. If authenticity is your north star, but you remain in a friend group that demands constant pretence, friction arises. Instead of forcing yourself to fit in, look for circles that appreciate you as you are. The same logic applies to job settings. If you believe in fairness but your workplace engages in unethical practices, you might question whether to stay or seek alternatives. Such decisions are not easy, but living out your values prevents the slow burn of self-betrayal.

Accountability can help you stay on track. Perhaps a close friend or coach can act as a sounding board when you face tricky decisions. "Does this choice honour what I claim to believe?" they might ask, nudging you to reflect. Regular self-checks, like journaling or monthly personal reviews, also keep you mindful. At these intervals, compare your activities with your stated values. If you spot discrepancies, decide what adjustments to make.

As you align actions with values, you cultivate greater serenity. Instead of running on autopilot, making random choices dictated by convenience or peer pressure, you consciously choose a direction. That clarity enhances your sense of identity. In turn, others view you as consistent and reliable, which typically attracts those who share or admire your guiding principles. This synergy expands your self-connection into your outer world, reinforcing that a life of integrity is deeply fulfilling.

The Role of Self-Reflection in Personal Growth

Self-reflection is like an internal mirror, showing you who you are now and nudging you toward who you could become. Without it, you may navigate life on autopilot, repeating habitual reactions or clinging to outdated assumptions. Taking regular intervals to look within, examining your actions, thoughts, and emotions, helps you consciously evolve, improving how you interact with yourself and others.

A straightforward way to practise reflection is journalling. Set aside ten minutes every day or week to jot down major moments, irritations, or joys. Rather than listing events superficially, explore how they affected you. Did you feel proud or uneasy? Why might that be? Over time, patterns emerge: You see which activities boost your mood, which relationships energise or drain you, and which triggers set off your anxieties. By capturing these details, you gather clues about where you might want to focus changes.

Reflection also applies to goal setting. If you harbour aspirations, say you want to learn a musical instrument or adopt a healthier lifestyle, ask yourself how you have progressed over the past month. Have you taken concrete steps or procrastinated? This method helps you cut through self-delusion. Instead of vaguely complaining that you have no time, you pinpoint whether you are truly trying or letting other priorities overshadow your objectives. Honesty paves the way for recalibration.

Self-Connection: The Foundation of All Relationships

Look back not only on the day's events but also on how you responded to conflicts. Suppose you had a tense conversation with a colleague. Ask yourself: "What triggered my reaction? Could I have listened more carefully?" This is not about self-blame but about discovering alternative ways to handle future tension. You may notice that you speak sharply when feeling insecure. Next time, you can address your insecurities first, defusing the need for defensive words. Over repeated reflections, you refine your emotional responses, forging more harmonious interactions.

Self-reflection also stops you from clinging to an old identity that no longer suits you. Perhaps you saw yourself as unfit for leadership, but circumstances changed, and you led a project successfully. Without reflection, you might continue passing up leadership opportunities out of habit. Taking a moment to appreciate how you rose to the challenge can free you from a limiting self-image. By admitting, "I handled that well," you break old narratives and open yourself to bigger roles.

Ensuring your reflections result in tangible progress can mean outlining small action points. If you notice you often interrupt others, vow to practise mindful listening in at least one group meeting the following week. If your reflection reveals a neglected friendship, resolve to reach out for a brief check-in. By converting insights into steps, you transform introspection into self-improvement.

In the end, self-reflection is not about dwelling on mistakes. It is about gleaning lessons from them. As you track your emotional patterns, refine your communication, and confront outdated beliefs, you move forward with fresh clarity. You remain open to growth rather than feeling stuck in cycles of repetition. That ongoing evolution enriches all facets of your life, from how you treat yourself to the way you respond to loved ones. In short, self-reflection fosters growth that is both intentional and nourishing for your relationships and your spirit.

Overcoming Inner Critics: Building Inner Support

Your inner critic might be that voice whispering you are not capable enough, not skilled enough, or not deserving of success. It can sabotage your self-confidence, overshadow your achievements, and lead you to underestimate your potential. Though it may masquerade as "keeping you humble," this negative self-talk often blocks progress and sours your mood. Recognising and redirecting this inner critic can transform your outlook and strengthen your self-connection.

Begin by naming the critic. Notice when thoughts like "You are not smart enough" or "You will fail anyway" creep in. Label them mentally as "inner critic" or something unique that lets you separate those thoughts from reality. By personifying the critic, you gain emotional distance. Rather than swallowing the negative commentary unchallenged, you say, "Ah, there is that critic. I hear it, but I do not have to believe it."

Next, examine the evidence. If your critic claims you are always messing up, recall times you succeeded or solved problems effectively. When your critic insists nobody cares about your opinions, remember instances where people sought your input or praised your ideas. This factual counterpoint weakens the critic's hold. You see that its

Self-Connection: The Foundation of All Relationships

statements are exaggerations, often rooted in fear rather than truth. Eventually, you train your mind to meet negative self-judgement with rational perspective.

Replacing harsh internal chatter with compassionate self-talk is another step. Instead of repeating, "I messed up, I am worthless," you might say, "I struggled today, but that does not define my worth." Affirmations can feel awkward initially, but they guide your neural pathways toward supportive thinking. Over time, your brain becomes more inclined to find workable solutions instead of wallowing in discouragement.

It also helps to track patterns. Sometimes, the critic yells loudest in specific scenarios, public speaking, dealing with an authority figure, or tackling unfamiliar responsibilities. Identifying triggers allows you to prepare coping strategies. If you know presenting in front of colleagues activates your critic, practise more thoroughly or visualise success. A prepared mind leaves less room for self-doubt. After each presentation, note what went well, however minor. Those highlights serve as ready ammunition against the critic's negativity next time.

Discussing these self-criticisms with a trusted friend or counsellor is beneficial. Sharing your negative inner scripts often reveals how unfair or distorted they are. People who know you well can offer a more balanced view of your strengths, reminding you that your critic is not all-powerful. By letting their affirmations in, you build an inner support system that counters negative messages. Some individuals even keep a "praise file," storing positive feedback or compliments for reference when feeling insecure.

Ultimately, you shift from a self-limiting to a self-supporting mindset. You might never silence the critic entirely, but you reduce it to background noise. In its place, you cultivate an inner cheerleader, reminding you of your resilience, your learning capacity, and your worthiness. This pivot from destructive introspection to encouraging self-talk grounds you in positivity. You stop sabotaging your own efforts and embrace challenges with renewed confidence. As that confidence grows, you see better outcomes in your relationships because you no longer let self-doubt overshadow your natural warmth and talents.

Cultivating Inner Peace: Practices for Emotional and Spiritual Well-being

Inner peace is a state of calm that shields you from the turbulence of everyday events. It does not mean you float through life unaffected; rather, you develop a reservoir of tranquillity that helps you respond constructively. Cultivating inner peace often involves tending to both emotional and spiritual dimensions, strengthening your sense of purpose and ability to handle life's twists.

One pathway lies in silent meditation or prayer. You set aside time to quiet external chatter and tune in to a deeper awareness. This can nurture spiritual growth, if that resonates with you, or simply offer a mental break. Slowly, you realise that your worth does not stem purely from achievements. You shift from a mindset that focuses on external validation to one that recognises inherent dignity. This foundation of peace then carries into daily tasks, making you less reactive and more centered.

Self-Connection: The Foundation of All Relationships

Affirmations and visualisations can complement these quiet practices. As you close your eyes, you might picture a serene location, a mountain top or a gentle ocean shore. Breathe steadily, imagining each exhale releasing tension. Then repeat affirmations like, "I am safe, I am calm," or "I face challenges with grace." Over time, such visual sessions deepen your sense of inner security. When stressors appear, you recall that internal sanctuary. It becomes simpler to remain composed, even in moments of chaos.

Gratitude exercises also raise your sense of peace. By listing three things each day that inspire thankfulness, a supportive friend, a comfortable home, or a skill you have improved, you remind yourself that life contains blessings. Even if you face obstacles, you do not lose sight of the good around you. This shift in focus softens negative rumination, aligning you with a more balanced emotional state.

Additionally, consider your spiritual perspective. Some find that connecting with nature, praying, or reflecting on universal truths fosters deeper peace. Others might explore philosophical readings. The essence is to tap into something that transcends mundane problems. If you believe in a higher power, set aside time to communicate or reflect, seeking guidance. Or you might find meaning in humanitarian efforts, acknowledging your part in a larger human family. Such expansions of viewpoint allow you to see life's troubles in a broader context, easing anxiety and self-absorption.

Another aspect is regulating emotional triggers. If you know that certain news feeds or social media accounts heighten tension, reduce your exposure. If angry rants or endless gloom from external sources disturb your calm, limit your interactions with them. Being selective about what you ingest mentally is just as important as monitoring your diet physically. This refined approach guards the serenity you work so hard to cultivate.

Over time, these practices integrate into your lifestyle. Inner peace becomes your default position. You greet challenges with an unhurried approach, ready to think or pray your way through them calmly. Although chaos can swirl around you, you hold a steady centre. This not only benefits your mental health but also influences others, showing that a peaceful demeanour in stressful moments is possible. You become an example of equanimity, and your relationships prosper as you foster calm rather than spread panic. In essence, cultivating inner peace infuses all parts of your life with steadiness and empathy, ensuring you engage with the world from a place of grounded compassion.

Embracing Your Journey: The Path to Self-Discovery

Self-discovery is not a single aha moment but a continuous unfolding. Each stage of life reveals new facets of who you are, from exploring early career choices to reassessing priorities in midlife. Embracing your journey means accepting that growth does not happen in a neat, linear fashion. It is a winding path, sometimes marked by surprises or setbacks that paradoxically deepen your understanding of your core self.

You start by letting go of the notion that you must have it all figured out. Many people pressure themselves to pick a straight line from youth to retirement. Yet life rarely stays so tidy. Perhaps you switch career fields after realising that your

Self-Connection: The Foundation of All Relationships

passion lies elsewhere, or you re-evaluate your beliefs after facing personal challenges. Rather than labelling these shifts as mistakes, view them as stepping stones that shape your identity. Each turn in the road can highlight aspects of yourself you did not know existed.

Self-discovery also thrives on curiosity. Instead of coasting in your comfort zone, try new experiences, join a local group, attempt a new skill, or immerse yourself in different cultural practices. Through these ventures, you see how you react to unfamiliar environments. Maybe an art class reveals a latent creative side, or a volunteering project awakens a drive for community leadership. By adopting a student's mindset, you remain open to transformation regardless of age.

Reflecting on your story helps integrate the lessons you learn. You might chart significant events, personal triumphs, heartbreaks, professional shifts, and note the common themes. Have you repeatedly sought freedom or thirsted for recognition? Recognising recurring patterns illuminates your deeper motivations. You can then decide whether you wish to reinforce those patterns or attempt a fresh direction. Gradually, this reflection helps you see that each chapter in your life provided essential knowledge.

While it is tempting to compare your progress to others, remember that each person's route is unique. Some might find their calling early on; others discover it unexpectedly later in life. A friend might marry young and settle down while you roam for years before feeling ready to commit. Neither path is superior. By letting go of external benchmarks, you reduce needless self-judgement. Instead, you focus on authenticity. Does each new choice align with your spirit, or does it pander to society's expectations?

As you embrace your evolution, do not disregard the power of setbacks. A lost opportunity might drive you to build resilience. A heartbreak might teach you deeper empathy. These experiences, though painful, often shape your character with a nuance that comfort alone cannot provide. Reflect on them as you do with successes, extracting wisdom about how to move forward more wisely. Over time, you accept that adversity can be a teacher, sharpening your sense of purpose.

Ultimately, your journey of self-discovery is a process of constant refining. You remain a work in progress, discovering new layers even when you think you have yourself figured out. This fluid approach fosters humility and keeps you flexible. You greet each chapter of life with readiness because you understand that change is the norm. By embracing this ever-evolving journey, you free yourself from self-imposed limits, stepping into each day with curiosity and a welcome for who you might become next.

In Conclusion

You have delved into the heart of self-connection, discovering how nurturing inner awareness and self-love positively affects every interaction you have. Through daily mindfulness, recognising your personal energy, and affirming your unique worth, you free yourself to engage with life authentically. This inner work lays the groundwork for the relationships you seek: stable, empathetic, and genuine.

Now, you will step back to see how these individual transformations ripple outward. The final chapter reveals

Self-Connection: The Foundation of All Relationships

how your choices and energy can influence society. Whether through kindness, volunteering, or mentorship, your positive spirit travels far beyond personal circles. You will see that the self-care you have practised is not only for your benefit but a source of light that brightens the world around you.

Chapter 10

Impacting the World: The Ripple Effect of Positive Connections

Every act of kindness or empathy you extend has the power to extend well beyond its initial target. Such is the ripple effect: your personal behaviour affects others, who, in turn, pass on positivity to the next circle of contacts. This final chapter focuses on how your growth can uplift society at large. By approaching relationships with responsibility, empathy, and mindful generosity, you become part of a greater wave of positive change.

These pages will highlight small steps, like daily acts of kindness, and broader initiatives, like mentoring or advocacy. Whether it is bridging cultural divides or volunteering in a local cause, you contribute to a chain reaction of goodwill. Recognising your influence counters feelings of helplessness in a seemingly vast, impersonal world. You realise that your personal evolution can transform not only you but also the communities you belong to, nurturing a world guided by mutual support and consideration.

The Concept of Social Responsibility in Relationships

Social responsibility is not confined to donating to charities or enacting grand legislation. It also appears in the micro-level interactions you have daily. Whenever you show up with integrity, empathy, and a willingness to share, you practise responsibility toward the broader community. Relationships become the conduit for these actions, where your small deeds of thoughtfulness can accumulate, leading to a more caring environment.

To start, see each personal connection as part of a larger puzzle. If you consistently spread positivity in your circles, encouraging neighbours, helping a stressed colleague, or guiding a friend through a tough patch, you are effectively sending out waves of kindness. Those individuals, feeling energised, may do the same for others. Over time, the effect escalates beyond your direct line of sight. You might never know the full extent of your contribution, but it is there, impacting moods, decisions, and other bonds.

Social responsibility in relationships also means being aware of how your words or actions might influence someone's day or sense of worth. A dismissive remark or casual insult can leave someone deflated, affecting how they treat the next person they meet. Conversely, a genuine compliment or an attentive ear can provide hope to a person in distress. Though you cannot shoulder responsibility for every dimension of another person's life, you can acknowledge that your behaviour counts.

Another angle is choosing to stand for fairness within your circle. Suppose you see a friend being unfairly blamed or overlooked. Standing up for them can shift the group dynamic. By calmly stating, "I think we should hear this person's viewpoint," or "They deserve credit for their effort," you invite justice and equality into your social space. In workplaces, this might translate into acknowledging the contributions of a colleague who is overshadowed. Each time you intervene, you strengthen an ethos of respect.

Of course, social responsibility includes setting boundaries with negativity. If you detect gossip or bullying in a group, deciding not to participate is itself a stance for decency. You need not preach; a simple refusal to engage often signals your convictions. Over time, others might follow suit, deterred from destructive talk. Your subtle actions can guide the community's moral compass, showing that courtesy and honesty are more valued.

Furthermore, bridging generational gaps exemplifies social responsibility. If an older neighbour struggles with new technology, offer a few minutes of help. Or if your younger relative is hunting for career advice, share resources or introduce them to a mentor you know. These small gestures break down barriers, illustrating that each of us can extend help beyond our immediate interests.

In the end, social responsibility means you see beyond personal gain, recognising your place in a connected network. Rather than seeing relationships as purely private affairs, you view them as opportunities to foster collective well-being. This shift in perspective encourages you to act conscientiously, trusting that your thoughtful engagements, however modest, can spark lasting, positive effects throughout your shared environment.

Building Bridges: Overcoming Divides Through Understanding

Divisions, whether shaped by social background, beliefs, or generational differences, hamper collective progress. You can be a bridge-builder, using empathy and curiosity to unite people who might otherwise remain apart. It begins with acknowledging that every person holds a unique viewpoint informed by their upbringing or experiences. By valuing that perspective, you reduce the threat of misunderstanding, forging pathways toward dialogue and cooperation.

One practical step is to initiate friendly, open conversations with those outside your immediate circle. If you notice someone from a different cultural context or social group, engage them politely. Ask questions about their experiences and viewpoints, and be ready to share your own. Sincere curiosity signals that you respect them. This is not about forcing consensus; it is about discovering shared ground within your differences.

Another method is to watch your language. Labels or sweeping statements about a particular group often fuel tension. If you are discussing a politically charged topic, avoid attacking or ridiculing those who disagree. Instead, phrase your ideas around how the current approach impacts daily life, inviting them to do the same. This style of discourse replaces combative "us versus them" talk with a spirit of exploration. People become less defensive when they sense you are truly aiming to understand.

Sometimes, bridging divides needs a collaborative project. Imagine a community garden or local volunteering campaign. When people with varied backgrounds labour side by side, they develop camaraderie. Shared tasks often breed mutual respect because each person's effort, regardless of identity or beliefs, contributes to a collective goal. Upon completion, individuals tend to see each other not as stereotypes but as dedicated partners. These positive interactions weaken preconceived barriers, forging new channels of friendship.

Patience is key. In many cases, differences run deep, shaped by generations of assumptions. You might feel frustration when progress crawls or when old prejudices reappear. Keep your focus on the gradual process rather than quick fixes. Just as trust is built through repeated affirmations, bridging divides takes multiple respectful exchanges. Each conversation or joint endeavour plants a small seed of better understanding.

If conflicts arise, and they likely will, approach them by emphasising your shared humanity. For instance, if someone mocks another group's struggles, respond by highlighting that we all face challenges in life, albeit in varied forms. Offer parallels or personal anecdotes that foster empathy. By invoking universal emotions, love for family, fear of harm, longing for a secure future, you root the discussion in feelings most people recognise. This makes it easier to find a common language.

Ultimately, building bridges is not about erasing differences but forming respectful bonds across them. You remind yourself and others that each person's journey has shaped their viewpoint. While you might continue to disagree on certain issues, that does not prevent you from seeing their dignity. Through consistent acts of listening, collaboration, and shared empathy, you open channels that broaden everyone's perspective. Over time, these connections can ripple outward, lessening the friction caused by ingrained divides and fostering a society better primed for cooperation and harmony.

The Role of Empathy in Societal Change

Large-scale progress depends on people caring enough to see beyond personal comfort and empathise with those facing challenges. Empathy prompts you to imagine life in someone else's shoes, urging you to transform that understanding into meaningful action. While policy and organisational frameworks matter, empathy is the emotional fuel that keeps social initiatives alive. Without it, well-intended programmes often lose momentum or become bureaucratic rather than humane.

It starts with listening to voices often overlooked. Perhaps a local community struggles with limited resources, or an elderly neighbour endures loneliness due to mobility issues. By engaging them sincerely, you see the emotional reality behind any statistic. Data might show rising costs or social isolation, but a direct conversation reveals what that means day to day, shuffling between food banks or spending hours without human contact. Empathy ensures you feel the weight of their situation, motivating you to support real improvements.

Empathy also transforms how you advocate for causes. When speaking about social or environmental issues, focusing solely on facts or figures can appear impersonal, failing to touch hearts. If you incorporate real stories, like how a family overcame hardship through community assistance or how a wildlife sanctuary saved an endangered species, your audience gains a tangible connection. They understand the human or ecological impact rather than seeing it as abstract policy. This bridging of facts and compassionate storytelling often prompts individuals who might otherwise remain indifferent to get involved.

On a smaller scale, empathy in day-to-day interactions changes your social environment. If a co-worker struggles with mental health, you might adjust your approach, offering regular check-ins or reducing the pressure where possible.

This practical empathy fosters an atmosphere that encourages open discussion of mental well-being, lessening the stigma that otherwise hides problems. Over time, your example can shift workplace norms, inspiring managers and team members to adopt similar supportive gestures.

Moreover, empathy can guide how you shape or evaluate social endeavours. If you run a local reading programme for children, you do not simply ask, "How many books are checked out?" You also wonder if the children feel encouraged. Do they experience reading as a joyful, enlightening act, or does it feel forced? By measuring the emotional dimension, you create programmes that genuinely connect with people, rather than ticking boxes. This emotional intelligence sets the stage for genuine growth and better results.

Empathy does not require that you fix every problem alone. It does ask that you acknowledge suffering or injustice, however big or small, and see it as relevant to you. In step with your abilities, you then take action, maybe through volunteering, fundraising, or spreading the word. Even short acts, like listening attentively to someone in pain, can spark a sense of hope that they are not invisible. Over time, empathy across a community becomes a collective force, changing how decisions are made, how resources are shared, and how future generations learn to treat one another.

Ultimately, empathy merges personal compassion with public responsibility. It reminds you that societal change does not rely only on officials or experts, but on everyone recognising shared humanity. When you remain open to the lived experiences of others, you keep the flame of collective goodwill burning. That warmth can galvanise efforts at every level, from quiet daily kindnesses to broader campaigns that profoundly shift societal values.

Volunteering and Community Service: Connecting Through Giving Back

Volunteering represents a direct way to convert your empathy and community spirit into practical outcomes. Whether you mentor students, clean up a local park, or distribute supplies at a shelter, your involvement helps solve problems while fostering genuine bonds among those involved. In a world often driven by personal ambition, volunteering highlights a different narrative: you share your time and skills with no demand for personal gain.

Choosing where to volunteer should align with your strengths or passions. If you enjoy reading, you might assist in a literacy programme. If you value nature, a local conservation project could energise you. This synergy between personal interests and social causes often sustains your commitment. Rather than viewing it as a charitable chore, you feel uplifted each time you contribute. The emotional satisfaction gained from aiding a cause resonates with your deeper values, reinforcing the cycle of giving.

Volunteering also shapes a support network among other volunteers. Working alongside people who share your dedication to a cause can lead to camaraderie. You swap stories, uplift each other when tasks feel heavy, and celebrate collective wins. This environment fosters new friendships. Sometimes, these friendships cross generational or cultural lines. You connect with people you might not otherwise have encountered, broadening your social circle and perspective.

Moreover, community service can enhance your skill set. Perhaps helping with event organisation hones your planning abilities, or tutoring fosters better communication techniques. If you find it gratifying, you might develop leadership qualities by coordinating bigger volunteer projects in the future. Employers also appreciate these experiences, seeing them as proof of your initiative and empathy. Indeed, volunteering might introduce you to potential mentors, job leads, or references who notice your work ethic and approachability.

Emotional growth is another benefit. When you share a conversation with someone who is homeless or befriend a child in a struggling household, you are humbled by perspectives outside your comfort zone. You see how real people are affected by broader social problems. That insight may feed your empathy further, spurring you to continue making a difference. It also fosters gratitude for any stability you enjoy, reminding you to handle your own life challenges with renewed resilience.

Lastly, volunteering can be flexible. You might give a few hours monthly, or if your schedule allows, you could commit to a weekly shift. Some who have limited time volunteer for short, high-impact events. Others might undertake remote tasks, like online mentoring or writing letters for a cause. The key is consistency, no matter the frequency. Ongoing involvement lets you form genuine connections with the community you serve, ensuring you make lasting contributions rather than occasional drops of help.

In the end, volunteering is about fellowship. You step outside self-focused routines, realising your potential to spark good in a society full of needs. Each bag of groceries you deliver, each hour you spend teaching, or each tree you plant leaves a tangible mark. More profoundly, you carry the spirit of service back into your daily life, influencing how you treat neighbours and strangers alike. When you see the tangible difference you make, you understand that sincere giving can transform both the community and your own heart.

The Global Tribe: Creating Connections Across Cultures

Your personal community might spread beyond your immediate area, especially in an age of online networks and global travel. Connecting with people across cultural backgrounds can broaden your perspective while promoting mutual respect. You realise that "tribe" is not limited to your neighbourhood or nationality; rather, it can form with individuals who share your principles or passions, regardless of where they live.

One straightforward approach is to embrace cultural exchanges, both virtual and in person. You could join online forums for language practice, watch documentaries about other societies, or plan trips that encourage real engagement with local traditions. By stepping away from touristy bubbles and interacting authentically, you gain a genuine sense of everyday life somewhere else. If you find acquaintances in that region, you might continue the friendship online, offering them a window into your world as well.

Collaboration on international initiatives also builds cross-cultural bonds. Maybe your workplace has a global project, or you join a volunteer programme in another country. Working toward shared objectives fosters camaraderie. You learn to navigate different work styles and time zones, refining your communication skills. Over time, new friendships emerge organically. You see that despite linguistic or cultural gaps, many core human concerns, family, livelihood, personal fulfilment, are universal.

Adopting a mindset of humility helps. If you visit a friend's cultural event, ask about the symbolism behind traditions without implying your own customs are superior. Listen more than you speak, let them explain the heritage and stories behind certain ceremonies or celebrations. If they offer you unfamiliar food, approach it with openness instead of squeamishness. By showing respect for differences, you invite them to be equally curious about your background. This reciprocity cements trust.

Technology also accelerates global tribes. Social media groups dedicated to specific interests, like sustainable living, classical music, or coding, can gather enthusiasts from every continent. If you participate with genuine contributions, you might form close bonds with people you never meet physically. That sense of community can be powerful, offering emotional support during challenges or celebrations of your successes, no matter the distance. Over time, some of these online friends might become real-life companions if travels align.

Of course, cross-cultural exchanges can involve misunderstandings. You might accidentally offend someone by not abiding by local etiquette, or they might misinterpret your words due to translation nuances. Approach these moments with a sense of patience and humour, ready to learn from mistakes rather than becoming defensive. Often, these small collisions become stepping stones to deeper awareness, giving you memorable lessons about perspective-taking.

Ultimately, the idea of a "global tribe" expands your sense of belonging. You carry not just your local group but a worldwide community of individuals with whom you share human values, moral visions, or creative energies. Through consistent curiosity, open discussion, and empathy, you discover that cultural barriers can be bridges to fresh insights. This unity across borders fosters a broader worldview, countering divisive notions by highlighting the shared humanity that binds us all.

Acts of Kindness: Small Actions, Big Impact

Acts of kindness might sound insignificant on the surface, yet they often create deeper effects. A simple gesture, like covering someone's coffee cost or writing a cheerful note, lifts your mood and the recipient's, inspiring a chain reaction. When individuals witness kindness, they are prompted to replicate it. The result is a subtle but powerful movement where a handful of warm gestures proliferate throughout a community.

In daily life, these moments of kindness take many forms. You might offer to carry groceries for an elderly neighbour or share a piece of advice with a colleague who looks overwhelmed. Paying attention to small details is key. If a co-worker seems silent and tense, a gentle inquiry, "Are you all right?", could be the bright spot in their day. Kindness does not always involve money or major time; often it is about empathy and a willingness to help spontaneously.

Kindness helps you as much as the receiver. Studies suggest that kind acts release positive neurochemicals, bolstering an overall sense of calm and satisfaction. You reinforce in yourself the idea that generosity is natural, which fosters greater self-esteem. Moreover, once you adopt kindness as a habit, you tend to notice more opportunities to lighten someone's burden. A synergy emerges: the more you do it, the more fulfilling it becomes, and your social environment responds by echoing that uplifting energy.

Another point about kindness is that it does not demand perfection. You can be kind amidst a busy schedule or on days when you feel stressed. Even if you cannot dedicate hours volunteering, a quick text of encouragement or a small donation can still make a difference. Focusing on the micro-acts breaks the misconception that kindness must be grand or time-consuming. Every small step counts. Over time, these gestures add up, shifting the tone of daily interactions from self-centred to collectively aware.

Receiving acts of kindness also teaches you humility and gratitude. If someone drives you home when your car breaks down or covers your meal when you forgot your wallet, you realise how good it feels to be on the receiving end. That experience can motivate you to pass it on, completing the kindness cycle. You see that none of us are entirely self-sufficient. Sometimes, support from a stranger or friend can turn a stressful situation around, reminding you that people do care.

Beyond personal circles, these acts of goodwill can expand. You can occasionally pay for someone's groceries if you have extra funds, or give away clothing you no longer need. If you want to involve others, you might organise a small challenge, encouraging your circle to share examples of kind gestures they performed in a week. These stories ignite more creativity, inspiring participants to think of different ways to spread positivity.

In essence, acts of kindness form the bedrock of a compassionate community. They disprove the notion that large-scale changes hinge on grand interventions alone. With consistent, small acts done by many, an underlying atmosphere of solidarity takes hold. When individuals habitually think, "What quick kindness can I offer here?" solutions to bigger challenges often follow, guided by the sense that helping each other is not an obligation but a natural, rewarding part of being human.

The Power of Mentorship: Guiding the Next Generation

Mentorship lets you shape the future by investing in the growth of someone younger or less experienced. It is not confined to the workplace. Perhaps you mentor a student in your neighbourhood or a friend's child interested in your profession. By sharing your insights and offering steady encouragement, you help them navigate opportunities and pitfalls that you faced in earlier days.

One way to initiate mentorship is to look for bright, curious individuals in your sphere. Maybe there is an intern at work who consistently asks thoughtful questions, or a teen in your neighbourhood who shows talent in arts or sports. Offer your guidance in a structured yet flexible manner, like meeting monthly or keeping a message channel open for their queries. They often appreciate a reliable figure they can approach for honest advice or resources. If they are hesitant, affirm that you are there when they are ready.

Good mentorship revolves around listening. Rather than shower them with your own experiences, ask them about their goals, challenges, and fears. Then, adapt your advice accordingly. Suppose a young mentee worries about choosing a career path. Rather than pushing your favourite route, ask about their interests, talents, and how they like to solve problems. Help them explore multiple possibilities. This approach fosters independence, where the mentee learns to think rather than rely on instructions.

Mentorship also involves modelling values. If you emphasise integrity, show them how you maintain honesty in difficult scenarios. Let them see how you handle disappointment or rebound from a missed opportunity. These real-life examples can be more influential than any lecture. They view resilience in action, realising that setbacks do not define a person's future unless they quit trying.

Your guidance need not be perfect; being transparent about your own missteps can be an invaluable lesson. Explain how you overcame a past challenge or learned from a failure. This normalises the idea that everyone stumbles at times, helping your mentee approach adversity without panic. In doing so, you become a trustworthy figure who does not pretend to have all the answers but stands ready to support them as they search for their path.

The effect of mentorship can last a lifetime, far beyond a single project or academic year. Many accomplished figures recall a mentor who believed in them when no one else did. Your words or small acts might sow seeds that your mentee nurtures into major achievements. Even if they take a different direction, the encouragement they received from you can instil self-belief. That self-belief then ripples into their relationships, further spreading positivity.

Finally, recall the mutual nature of mentorship. While you guide them, you often learn fresh perspectives. Younger people or novices might question the norms you have accepted for years, prompting you to rethink your methods or find a new spark of innovation. This exchange keeps you open-minded, bridging generational divides and renewing your own sense of purpose. Mentorship, then, is not only about imparting wisdom but also about staying curious, flexible, and attuned to the evolving world. You both emerge enriched, forging a bond that can continue growing as they mature into mentors themselves one day.

Advocacy and Social Change: Using Your Voice for Good

Advocacy means stepping up for a cause that resonates with your moral compass. Sometimes, you see an injustice or an overlooked need, and you decide to speak out. By raising awareness, you can influence policies or encourage others to join your mission. While it might feel daunting, advocacy stems from the same principles discussed throughout this book: empathy, responsibility, and a focus on positive impact.

You need not be an expert to advocate for something meaningful. Start by clarifying your stand: what problem do you see, and why does it matter? Maybe it is an environmental issue in your local community, a shortfall in your regional healthcare, or a pressing social concern. Gather factual information to ensure you communicate accurately. Then, share the story behind those facts, highlighting how real lives are affected. Storytelling helps listeners connect emotionally, going beyond mere statistics.

Choose appropriate platforms to voice your perspective. Online channels are accessible, but in-person speaking or direct conversations can be impactful as well. If you take the online route, use social media responsibly, focusing on respectful dialogue instead of heated debates. Tag relevant organisations or officials who can aid the cause. If you prefer live gatherings, attend town hall meetings, local forums, or even smaller community events. When addressing an audience, be clear on what you hope they will do: sign a petition, alter a behaviour, or support a local project. Presenting a defined action point transforms awareness into tangible steps.

Collaborations amplify your reach. Joining an existing group or coalition working on the same issue leverages collective knowledge and resources. You might find a local environmental club or a nationwide charity that welcomes volunteers for an upcoming campaign. By coordinating, you share responsibilities. One person might design flyers, another might host a fundraising event, and a third could liaise with local media. Working in unity also bolsters credibility, showing that this cause matters to multiple stakeholders, not just an isolated individual.

Expect resistance or indifference at times. Advocacy challenges entrenched interests or disrupts comfortable norms. People might downplay the need for change or claim your concerns are exaggerated. Rather than becoming discouraged, practice patience. Reiterate your message calmly, backed by respectful logic and, when suitable, heartfelt stories that underline the human dimension. Persistence can shift opinions gradually. Even if you only convert a few minds, those new supporters might convince others, building momentum over time.

It is also important to balance passion with self-care. Advocacy can be emotionally draining. You might see distressing stories or face negative responses. Take periodic breaks to recharge. Speak with supportive friends or mentors, reminding yourself that no single person can solve every challenge overnight. Your role is to do your part, however small, steering events toward a better outcome. This perspective nurtures resilience, helping you stay dedicated without succumbing to burnout or cynicism.

In the end, advocacy aligns personal conviction with public action. Rather than complaining about problems, you choose to influence the narrative. Your voice, be it large or modest, can be a catalyst for improvement. Each step you take encourages others to re-evaluate their stances, forging a wave of shared commitment. Together, those efforts shape the world into one where compassion, justice, and hope stand stronger.

Acts of Generosity: Sharing Resources for a Greater Good

Generosity goes beyond simple kindness; it reflects a willingness to share your resources, be they time, money, skills, or connections. By offering these assets to those in need, you contribute tangibly to uplifting them. This collaborative sense of distributing resources shifts society from a purely competitive framework toward a supportive one. People see that their well-being can be linked to the prosperity of others.

Monetary donations are one expression of generosity. You might donate to a cause dedicated to alleviating homelessness or supporting educational programmes. Regular, smaller contributions often prove more sustainable than large, infrequent sums. However, do not underestimate non-monetary gifts. If you have organisational skills, volunteer to coordinate a community fundraiser. If you own a vehicle, offer transport assistance to neighbours who struggle with errands. These gestures address immediate needs while forming deeper community ties.

Generosity also thrives on practical solutions. If your workplace discards surplus materials that could be reused, such as old computers or furniture, arrange for donation to schools or shelters, if policies allow. By transforming waste into a useful resource, you encourage a cycle of reusability that benefits everyone. Over time, these resource-sharing habits can trickle into daily life: you might trade or lend tools with neighbours rather than buying new gear. Such cooperative acts reduce costs, cut waste, and strengthen trust within your environment.

While it is fulfilling to see direct results, generosity does not always reveal immediate rewards. Sometimes you might give anonymously, or support causes overseas, where the beneficiaries remain unseen. In these cases, trust that your offering reaches people who can put it to good use. If you wish for more transparency, you can research charities to confirm they are reputable. Reading reports or volunteering on-site can help you grasp how donations are distributed, easing any doubts about their impact.

Generosity is not about depleting yourself or showing off. If you give beyond your means or to gain admiration, resentment or pride may surface. Instead, aim for a balanced approach. Contribute in a way that feels meaningful but does not compromise your household's well-being. If finances are tight, devoting time or skills can be equally valuable. Your aim is to nurture an ethos of shared care, not to erode your ability to manage your personal responsibilities.

Over time, your contributions can form a ripple of collective generosity in your circles. You might discover friends become inspired by your approach, deciding to share their resources too. Small actions multiply. A few donated books become an entire library for children in underfunded schools when multiple donors unite. By persistently choosing generosity, you foster a climate where people believe in supporting one another, reversing the idea that life must be an unceasing competition for scarce resources.

Ultimately, acts of generosity reflect faith in communal strength. You trust that pouring resources into a common pool, be it knowledge, finances, or time, helps raise the baseline of security and opportunity for all. Through these unselfish gestures, you leave a lasting positive impression on your neighbours, colleagues, or even unknown beneficiaries. While you may not see every outcome, the uplifting effect remains, contributing to a more caring community that stands on the foundation of shared abundance rather than fear of scarcity.

Paying It Forward: Creating a Cycle of Positive Impact

Paying it forward occurs when you receive a kindness and decide to pass kindness along to someone else, often without expecting anything in return. This concept symbolises a chain of benevolence that can expand through any group or town. By joining that chain, you remind people that gratitude is best expressed not only through thanks to the giver but through renewed generosity to the next person in need. Little by little, this approach sows seeds of hope, reminding us that good deeds do not have to end with the initial exchange.

Examples of paying it forward come in everyday contexts. Suppose someone covers your coffee bill, leaving you a note that says, "If you can, do something nice for another person today." You might later see a passer-by struggling with heavy bags, so you pause to help. You felt uplifted by that initial gesture, so you spontaneously share that uplift with someone new. Now, that person, recalling your help, may later assist a colleague or a neighbour.

You can also institutionalise paying it forward. Some cafes allow you to buy an extra drink in advance, redeemable by anyone short on money. Similar initiatives arise in restaurants or community shops. This structure encourages an ongoing loop of philanthropy. Rather than a one-off gift, it becomes a collective invitation for customers to pass on kindness to strangers. People step in, witnessing that small contributions can significantly brighten someone's day.

Paying it forward can manifest at work, too. If a senior colleague trains you patiently, you might mentor a junior employee in turn. You do not necessarily repay your own mentor directly; perhaps they have no need or do not want to accept any gift. Instead, you continue the cycle by guiding someone else. This tradition of offering help fosters a supportive workplace culture that multiplies as each newly skilled individual feels compelled to help others.

Educating children about paying it forward leaves a profound legacy. You might share stories of how a small, kind act triggered a wave of goodness. Encouraging them to practise simple deeds, like sharing their lunch or comforting a classmate, can shape their sense of community and empathy. This shapes a generation that grows up viewing kindness not as a random gesture but as a chain that unites everyone.

Critics sometimes wonder if these small acts genuinely address larger societal problems. While paying it forward might not solve systemic injustices on its own, it is a gentle yet meaningful reminder that empathy is alive and well. When aggregated, these acts foster community resilience, ensuring that individuals never feel wholly abandoned by society. If combined with activism, policy changes, or collective projects, paying it forward adds an emotional dimension that humanises broader initiatives.

At its essence, paying it forward embodies the trust that good can spark more good. You break the typical transaction model, where every favour is swapped or repaid directly, replacing it with a ripple effect of kindness. You give to an unknown future recipient, confident that generosity has a life of its own once released. That cycle, sustained by everyday individuals, demonstrates the power of conscious choice in shaping communal well-being. Far from being idealistic fantasy, paying it forward stands as a practical phenomenon, offering hope that each person's small positive act can accumulate into something far greater.

In Conclusion

As you reach the final chapter's end, you see that your personal growth, once rooted in self-awareness, can extend beyond private realms to transform your neighbourhood, workplace, and global community. Every kind gesture, mentoring moment, or stance you take for societal good triggers ripples that enrich countless lives. The question of how best to use your influence never looms too large because even modest, well-intentioned deeds matter.

Next, you come to the closing reflections of this book. You have studied how each element of connection, family ties, friendships, romantic bonds, professional relationships, and social responsibilities can be uplifted through self-understanding and compassion. In the final word, you will gather these threads and see how your journey weaves into the broader human tapestry (word restricted, sorry), reaffirming that each choice you make resonates well beyond your personal circle.

Final Word

This book has guided you across different dimensions of connection, from recognising the influences of your family heritage to forging your workplace identity and eventually projecting your positive impact into society. You might have begun this journey wanting healthier bonds with friends or a calmer family life, but you end it knowing these relationships reflect deeper shifts within yourself.

Nurturing self-awareness, boundaries, or gratitude, all those practices covered reveals you can shape relationships by revising your inner dialogue, daily habits, and emotional presence. You see that being calm in a heated debate depends on your ability to recognise triggers and respond with empathy. You discover that upholding boundaries in a draining environment is an extension of respecting your own dignity. Through consistent effort, you remake your internal landscape into one that promotes stable, authentic interactions.

You also explored how every gesture, even a small one, radiates outward. It might begin with a simple word of encouragement to a neighbour or a thoughtful act for a colleague. The chain reaction of positivity moves forward, lifting others, who then carry that energy to further circles. In that sense, the power you hold is not limited by the boundaries of your personal life or your desk at work. Your capacity to be a beacon can ripple through society, comforting those you never meet and inspiring those you never see.

Final Word

With these insights in hand, you can approach life more intentionally. If challenges still arise, as they will, you know that every test can be tackled with mindful presence, renewed empathy, or a fresh boundary. Likewise, your growth in love relationships, friendships, and family matters stems from the self-connection you have so diligently cultivated. As you continue walking this path, remember that each step carries you closer to the version of you who engages the world from wholeness rather than fear or compulsion.

A time may come when you need to revisit these concepts, refining what you have learned or seeking new angles as your circumstances evolve. Perhaps you will find yourself sharing these lessons with a friend who seeks guidance, passing on the knowledge through daily conversations or deeper mentorship. In this manner, the flame of understanding travels onward, illustrating how one person's personal evolution can serve many.

Hold on to the confidence that you can harmonise your inner world with the outer relationships that define your life. You deserve to experience relationships that reflect respect, kindness, and a spirit of mutual uplift. Thank you for journeying through these pages. May you walk forward encouraged and alert, shining your light in every environment you enter and trusting in the profound potential of aligned and compassionate human connection.

The End

Printed in Great Britain
by Amazon

61519036R00147